THE ANXIOUS GARDENER'S BOOK OF ANSWERS

THE ANXIOUS GARDENER'S BOOK OF ANSWERS

TERI DUNN CHACE

ILLUSTRATIONS BY COLLEEN COOVER

Timber Press
Portland • London

Published in 2012 by Timber Press, Inc.

The Haseltine Building
133 S.W. Second Avenue, Suite 450
Portland, Oregon 97204-3527
timberpress.com

2 The Quadrant
135 Salusbury Road
London NW6 6RJ
timberpress.co.uk

Printed in the United States of America

Library of Congress Cataloging-in-Publication Data

Dunn Chace, Teri.
The anxious gardener's book of answers/Teri Dunn Chace; illustrations by
Colleen Coover.
       p. cm.
Includes bibliographical references and index.
ISBN 978-1-60469-235-8
1. Gardening. I. Coover, Colleen. II. Title.
SB450.97.D86 2012
635dc23   2011027108

A catalog record for this book is also available from the British Library.

Heartfelt thanks to Tom Fischer, Roger B. Swain, Kathleen Pyle, Alan Chace, Wes and Tristan Dunn, Barbara and Heru Lamb-Hall, Elizabeth Golding, Rosemary Blau and Linda Christie, Larry Levinger, Sarah Rutledge Gorman, and Cassandra Wilson.

Dedicated to my gardening mentor, the late W. C. (Bill) Frase, who always advised me to be thorough, constant, neat, and patient—good advice for gardening, book writing, and living!

NTENTS

introduction

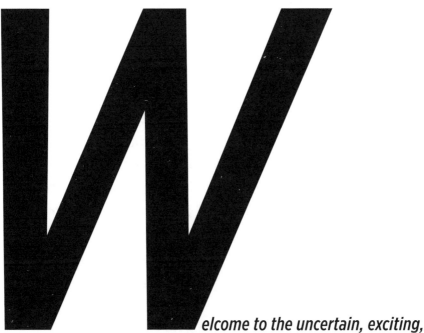

Welcome to the uncertain, exciting, fraught, gratifying world of gardening. Whether you are a complete newbie or have enjoyed some success in your yard and are now expanding your ambitions, the fact remains that it's a wide-open field. There's so much to do and so much to learn. So many plants, so many choices, so many creative ideas. So many gardening books, magazines, catalogs, websites, and chat rooms.

We live in an age of exploding information. The upside is obvious: you can look up almost anything you might want to know—about plants; about techniques and projects and design schemes; about care and coping with pests and diseases and harvesting. The downside is also apparent: so much information can be downright overwhelming. What if you discover facts that contradict each other or don't match what you observe in your own yard?

First, thank you and congratulations for buying this book. A book remains arguably the best way to educate yourself quietly and contemplatively, at your own pace. You can thumb through and pause where something catches your interest, refer to the table of contents, or browse the index. You can set it down and return later, when you know more or your questions are clearer. The information here is deliberately brief and pragmatic, so you won't feel like you're drinking it through a fire hose.

Let me also add that because everyone is so busy nowadays, I emphasize sensible and efficient tactics and advice that save time and heartache. And because there is an ever-growing interest in—and, to be frank, an urgent need for—gardening practices that are organic and have a low impact on the environment, you'll find that theme *as well. My goal is to help you become a more efficient, savvier gardener, while having fun along the way. That's how it should be.*

For most of us, the days are gone when older, more experienced gardeners mentored young or new ones. The loss of this continuum of practical and inspirational help is a grievous one indeed. The gentle or bossy instructions and advice of your gardening grandmother or nurturing neighbor were valuable precisely because they were not overwhelming. They knew what they were talking about because they had once been in your shoes—gaping at the disease-ridden rosebush leaves, wondering why the peony wasn't blooming, or ruing the weeds. They understood your worries, answered your questions, and passed on their gardening wisdom in calm and concise tones.

Calm? You know that "oops" or "uh-oh" sinking feeling, but you may not even trust yourself, never mind navigating your way to answers you can trust. Something in your garden has gone awry for some unknown reason, or you could have done this or that differently—right? Today's smaller yards and decks or patio container-based gardens mean there is a narrower margin of error. You don't want to screw up what little gardening space you have. You want beautiful, productive, healthy displays. You don't want to ruin everything.

Relax. As your gardening grandmother and nurturing neighbor might have told you if they were here now: plants are fairly forgiving. They want to live. Everything will be all right. Mistakes can almost always be corrected, or you can learn good lessons from your errors. Dear anxious gardener: please relax, regroup, learn as you go— and enjoy your garden.

HOW TO USE THIS BOOK

Start with the table of contents. Individual chapters address the most common garden topics in alphabetical order, and within them, the most frequent garden mistakes or "oh, no" moments. Likely you will recognize familiar issues, situations, and questions and can get some help and reassurance. You will pick up ideas and information that show how prevention is key, and you will become a better steward of your home landscape and a better gardener going forward. To use this as a reference book, consult the detailed index, which can send you directly to plants, problems, or projects of specific or immediate interest.

*Be patient as you browse, and feel free to read
several entries on topics that concern you and your garden.
A broader picture should emerge: Most mistakes
are not disasters, and it is within your power to right a
gardening wrong.*

*It is my fervent hope that the nuggets of information and
wisdom I share will lead you to feel less worried. You may
be inclined or compelled to continue your education
or search for further information (even returning to the
overwhelming Internet), but do yourself and your garden
a favor and walk that path. Walk, don't run. Your garden
will prosper under the care of a more patient gardener who
is now confident that everything will be all right.*

BULBS

GET A HANDLE ON BULB SUCCESS— BEFORE, DURING, AND AFTER THE DISPLAY.

Planting bulbs upside-down

While you would never put a living plant into the ground upside-down, you might make this somewhat embarrassing, but all-too-common, mistake if you've never planted bulbs or are planting a kind that's new to you. After all, bulbs are dormant, and there are no stems, foliage, or crisp white roots to clearly clue you in to which end is up. If there is a pointy end, you might guess the roots will eventually emerge from there—and, alas, you will be wrong. For the vast majority of bulbs, from tulips to wee snowdrops, the pointy end is up.

THE RIGHT WAY TO DO IT Growth is most efficient when you plant a bulb roots down and growing end up. In the case of most popular bulbs, this is generally easy to see. Like a store-bought onion, the top (where all new growth will emerge) is pointy, and the bottom—the basal plate—is flat or flattish. If the orientation is not immediately obvious, such as with some crocuses or ranunculus, peer at each bulb more carefully and you should be able to figure it out. Sometimes you'll even spot tiny dried roots adhering to the basal plate.

IF I GOOFED, CAN I FIX IT? If you planted only a few bulbs and you realize your error before the ground freezes, dig them up and replant them. The prospect of digging up an entire bed of incorrectly planted bulbs, however, may be daunting. Fortunately, plants have a will to live. Upside-down bulbs, if otherwise planted in good prepared soil at the correct depth, will still generate roots, and the emerging stems will manage to make a U-turn in order to reach the world above. They will probably emerge aboveground a bit later but will likely still be strong plants.

Planting bulbs at the wrong depth

You may be new to growing bulbs, or perhaps you're planting some that are new to you. Instructions and advice abound, and you do your best and get them into the ground. And then you have your doubts. Soon after planting, you read the instructions with more care or hear conflicting information, or a more experienced gardener chides your methods. Maybe you planted them too shallowly, in which case rodents will dig them up, or winter will freeze and kill your bulbs. Or maybe you planted them too deeply, and when spring comes they will never make the long trip to the surface. The display you so eagerly anticipated will be a bust.

THE RIGHT WAY TO DO IT Generally speaking, planting bulbs twice as deep as they are long is an effective, easy-to-remember strategy. If you have light, sandy soil, set them a little deeper; if you have clay, shallower is better. The important thing is to get them down in the ground deeply enough so that any freeze-thaw cycles won't heave them out, and they can get the chilling period they need to develop properly.

IF I GOOFED, CAN I FIX IT? If you are pretty sure planting depth is the issue, replant the bulbs promptly, or start over with new ones, and follow the twice-as-deep guideline.

WHAT ELSE?

Bulbs may fail to put on a good show for a variety of reasons. Among them: they were poor quality; you picked ones not adapted to your climate or not hardy enough to survive your winters; you planted them in terrible or waterlogged soil; you planted them in a site with too much or not enough sun; squirrels or other pests ate them (tulip bulbs are bonbons for squirrels); you planted something over them or they encountered some obstruction on their way up; or road salt, weedkiller, or another harmful substance filtered into their area. Finally, be sure to press a bulb into the soil so the basal plate at the bottom, where roots generate, can come into contact with the soil. An air pocket under a bulb may mean it will simply dry out, not grow or show.

18

Cutting back post-bloom bulb foliage

It's your first season growing spring-flowering bulbs, and you had a delightful show. What a lovely sight after the long, cold, barren winter. But now spring is in full swing, and you've been to the garden center and tucked in some annuals to keep things colorful as the bulb show subsides and before the surging perennials come into bloom—and those fading bulb plants look dreadful. You don't want to yank them out, so you simply chop off the floppy, yellowing leaves. Then, too late, you learn you were supposed to let the bulb foliage die back at its own rate because it was sending starch reserves down into the bulbs to fuel next year's show. Oops.

You may even have seen that some gardeners fold over the fading, floppy leaves and cinch them with a string or a rubber band. This doesn't look great, but it indicates to passersby that the resident gardener is not a neglectful slob. However, this tack is not optimal either, as it constricts or halts the refueling process.

THE RIGHT WAY TO DO IT The best solution is to tolerate the unsightly mess as it runs its course, but disguise the scene with strategically placed annuals or garden decor. Remove totally faded leaves, but do not yank, as you may inadvertently dislodge the bulb. A pair of pruners or even sharp scissors will do the trick.

IF I GOOFED, CAN I FIX IT? There's not much you can do this year. But next spring, as the plants begin to re-emerge, give them a boost. Use bulb food and apply it according to label directions. Also, resolve to let nature take its full course that season. If you try it and the show is still lousy, plan to buy and plant new bulbs.

Planting bulbs in the wrong spot

You had a nice vision last fall. A luxuriant blue carpet of crocuses under the evergreens in the backyard, or a rainbow of tulips along your driveway, or a frill of cheerful yellow-and-orange daffodils against the front of the house. But the beautiful scene fizzled. The backyard has dusty, dry soil (something you didn't notice last fall) and too much shade. The tulips didn't come up at all. And rain and snow have made a sodden mess of the daffodil bed. Bulbs are supposed to be relatively tough—at least the popular ones—and yet you seem to have given them a bad home and they are sulking.

THE RIGHT WAY TO DO IT Generally speaking, bulbs prosper in sunny locations in fertile, well-drained ground. Any spot that has poor, quick-draining, gritty, or sandy soil—or, conversely, is waterlogged—is bad for them. In dry soil, bulbs just dry out. In wet soil, they rot. As for exposure, they can be grown under shade of deciduous trees because they'll get enough sun before those fully leaf out, but it's bound to be too dark under evergreen trees.

Your best bet is to plant your bulbs in an open area of loamy, fertile soil that is neither too wet nor too dry—and that means neither too wet nor too dry over the winter months, too.

IF I GOOFED, CAN I FIX IT? Dried-out or rotted bulb plantings probably cannot be rescued, unfortunately. By the time you take note of their disappointing performance, it may be too late. Bulbs that have spent only one season in dense shade could still have some life in them and may be transplanted.

Dig up any stalwart survivors while they are still small or short, before they bloom, and gently transplant them to a better spot. Hope for the best—if not this season, maybe next year.

Planting old or dried-out bulbs

No gardener can be expected to take care of every detail every time, especially during the busy planting seasons of spring and fall. Sometimes unplanted bulbs turn up, forlorn and forgotten in a box or bag. They should have gone into the ground in the fall, had their obligatory winter-chilling period underground, and burst forth into glorious bloom the following spring. Because they have not followed this prescribed trajectory, they may have dried out, frozen, or molded or rotted in storage, and there is no possible rescue. This is the worst-case scenario.

The best-case scenario is they still have some vitality, despite neglect or abuse. Perhaps your basement or garage is not exposed to freezing temperatures and they are still alive and even properly chilled. Maybe brave little green growing tips are emerging.

THE RIGHT WAY TO DO IT You can try forcing found bulbs in decent condition into indoor bloom. Tulips, daffodils, and hyacinths are usually amenable. They'll have a chance if they've been cooling for 10 or so weeks (if fewer, you should wait). Pot them in light potting mix; water conservatively; put in a cool, dry, protected place; and keep an eye on them. If they start growing, move them into a bright room where you'll remember to water them more often and get to admire their eventual show.

In the future, if you must ever store bulbs on purpose, remember they can be kept in any dry, dark place where temperatures are above freezing but no higher (for most) than 42 to 48 degrees Fahrenheit. Most refrigerators are not cold enough. Keep them in a box or bag (but not in a plastic bag, which traps moisture and leads to rot).

IF I GOOFED, CAN I FIX IT? Bulbs that have spent more than one winter in storage, even good storage, are unlikely to grow and bloom well. Toss them on the compost pile.

CHEMICAL WARFARE

DEPLOY PESTICIDES AND HERBICIDES CORRECTLY TO GET THE RESULTS YOU WANT.

Misusing pesticides

Pesticides, as you know, are poisons. But when something—aphids? whiteflies? or are they spider mites?—attacks plants, some gardeners turn homicidal and grab a spray can.

Later, you feel uncertain or remorseful. Not regret for the critters you hopefully killed, but for your tactics. Was that product labeled for use on that sort of plant and for that sort of pest? Will that chemical harm honeybees or poison your soil? Will your peppers be safe to eat?

THE RIGHT WAY TO DO IT Always find out exactly which pest is marring your precious plants. If you can't tell because the insects are so tiny, or you don't have reference books or the patience for online research, try taking an afflicted plant (or a piece of it) to your local garden center or an experienced neighborhood gardener.

24

Ask for advice. Read labels—the fine print includes the information on which chemical is approved for which insect pests and how to properly apply the product. Bear in mind that organic or botanical pesticides are not necessarily nontoxic or totally safe (for example, pyrethrins, derived from a relative of the common garden mum, kill honeybees).

Proper timing (in the mornings when the pests may congregate), proper amounts (too much or too little won't get you the desired results), and proper methods (it's often good practice to treat the undersides of the leaves) are all important. In the future, keep an eye on all vulnerable plants so pests don't get out of hand. Best to nip problems early.

IF I GOOFED, CAN I FIX IT? If your second thoughts occur the same day you wantonly sprayed, hose down the plants thoroughly. In the process, you just may eradicate the pests, at least temporarily. Read—belatedly—the label. You may be relieved to discover that your chemical becomes harmless fairly quickly. Rotenone, varieties of Bt spray, and neem all break down in sunlight. If your homicidal spraying spree wasn't heavy-handed, the plants and garden may weather it; alas, even the pests might. If they return, you can explore alternative or organic combat.

Misusing weedkiller

What a wonderful thing weedkiller can be. It turns aggressive, in-the-way, unattractive weeds into withered, dead victims with gratifying skill and speed. They can be yanked out, mowed down, or overplanted

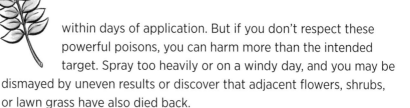within days of application. But if you don't respect these powerful poisons, you can harm more than the intended target. Spray too heavily or on a windy day, and you may be dismayed by uneven results or discover that adjacent flowers, shrubs, or lawn grass have also died back.

THE RIGHT WAY TO DO IT First, choose the right herbicide for the job. This means knowing what you want to kill (dandelions, crabgrass, clover, something else?) and shopping with care to find a product whose label states it is effective against the target.

Next, choose the right applicator and method. For weeds growing out of cracks in your walkway, a handheld spray bottle may be all you need. For larger areas, you may have to use a larger pump sprayer, which may require you to mix a concentrate with water before heading out to do battle. Be conservative. It's better to mix up a small batch and make refills as needed. If you are using a granular product, follow label advice with care, especially the instructions about applying it evenly.

Finally, protect yourself. Wear long pants, a long-sleeved shirt, a hat, rubber boots (easier to wash than work boots) and gloves, plus eye protection. Afterward, throw the clothes in the wash and shower with plenty of soap.

IF I GOOFED, CAN I FIX IT? If you applied a weedkiller too heavily, or in error, and you realize this pretty quickly, wash it all away as best you can. If it turns out you killed or harmed plants you didn't mean to, well, they aren't going to come back to life. Cut away the dead parts or dig up and get rid of the unintended victims, and chalk it up to a hard-earned lesson in herbicide application.

26

Injuring good plants with weedkiller

It's not that you don't know which plants are weeds, or that you didn't buy the right weedkiller. Instead, you sprayed a little too liberally, or the day was a bit breezy, and some of the spray hit good plants. Half the rosebush is scorched, it seems, or several perennials near the sprayed area have given up the ghost.

THE RIGHT WAY TO DO IT Never spray on a windy day, not even a slightly breezy one. Protect plants adjacent to the targeted spray area. Temporarily shroud them with a tarp, an old towel, a burlap sack, an upended paper bag, old pots, strategically placed plywood scraps— anything. Being cut off from light and air for a few minutes, hours, or even a whole day won't harm them.

IF I GOOFED, CAN I FIX IT? It depends. If you catch the contamination right away—in other words, realize your mistake as you see the drifting spray hitting the nearby plants—stop. Hose off the valuable plants and put up a barrier, then resume.

If the damage has been done, the plant or branches are not going to green up again. The roots may survive, depending on the chemical and the extent of the exposure. Try chopping out the damaged and dead parts and waiting to see if your good plant recovers. If it doesn't, you'll have to take it out and replace it.

WHAT ELSE?

Herbicide damage usually shows as brown or withered plant parts, but other things can also cause this, like road salt, drought (or sporadic or no watering), and poor soil. If you are observant and honest, you should be able to identify what has harmed your plants and take steps to make life better for them.

COMPOSTING

GENERATE YOUR OWN "BLACK GOLD" EASILY AND EFFICIENTLY.

Adding oils, meats, and other no-no's

Many gardeners have taken too literally the instructions to put kitchen scraps into their compost pile. You or someone in your household has thrown the ribs from last weekend's barbecue onto the pile, or oily salad greens or a chicken carcass have found their way in. Worst of all is pet debris—cat or dog waste or fur.

All of these are bad for your compost pile. Meats and oils do not break down well, and they spoil, smell rotten, and add nothing beneficial. Because cats and dogs are not vegetarians, their droppings contain meat products and do not belong in your compost pile. (This does not mean you can clean the bird or guinea-pig cage and toss in that stuff; although these pets qualify as vegetarians, their waste may contain diseases or organisms that the compost pile may not be hot enough to kill.)

30

Another important reason not to add the wrong stuff? A smelly compost pile can attract unwanted pests, including rats, crows or seagulls, raccoons, and skunks. This is a surefire way to turn yourself—and your nearby neighbors—against composting.

THE RIGHT WAY TO DO IT Add only true nitrogen-rich green materials, such as organic, vegetable, or fruit products, items, or waste to your compost pile. No exceptions. Also, crush eggshells, break up corncobs, and chop bigger items into small pieces to speed breakdown.

IF I GOOFED, CAN I FIX IT? Assuming the offending items haven't been buried deep in the pile, and depending on how squeamish you are, you can retrieve them and throw them away in your household garbage. The sooner you do this, the better. Make the project less disgusting by wearing rubber gloves, and be sure to wash up well afterward. Then scold the offender, review composting rules with your family, and post a reminder at the pile.

Neglecting to layer your compost pile

Diehards may disagree, but composting is not overly difficult. That said, doing it wrong—particularly, not layering properly—not only fails to yield good, rich black-gold compost, it has other drawbacks. Poorly layered compost operates excruciatingly slowly, and the pile develops an unpleasant, ammonia-like smell. Most novices who get these disappointing results are putting in only nitrogen-heavy or green materials, such as kitchen scraps and yard debris.

THE RIGHT WAY TO DO IT Composting works best when a pile has a balance of green and brown, or high-carbon, materials. High-carbon favorites that are usually easy to come by include straw (not hay, which harbors weed seeds), dry leaves (run a lawn mower back and forth over a pile to shred them beforehand), and even wood chips.

There are recipes and formulas, and some people even buy a special starter with beneficial microorganisms to spur the natural processes. But a simple 1:3 ratio—1 part green to 3 parts brown—is attainable and always successful. Keep some brown stuff near your pile and throw generous handfuls on top of each green delivery.

Remember that oxygen is also important. It allows the naturally occurring microorganisms to break down the materials you toss in. Poke holes in and stir up the layered pile occasionally with a stick or shovel. Don't worry about messing up the layers; this isn't a chocolate cake.

IF I GOOFED, CAN I FIX IT? Yes. Start adding brown materials. An easy solution is to buy a bale of straw and set it next to the pile so it's always handy and you don't forget it. Chopped-up fall leaves are also good. Piles that are covered work better and faster, too. A lid or tarp holds in heat and helps keep the moisture level constant. A pile that is too dry (exposed) or too damp (rained on) will take forever to break down.

32

Slowing down the process

Composting should not be an out-of-sight, out-of-mind gardening project, but neither should it be something you fuss over every day. Neglect can slow or thwart breakdown. Common examples of neglect are letting the pile dry out, forgetting to stir or turn it occasionally, and composting in too much shade. All of these practices yield poor results.

THE RIGHT WAY TO DO IT The composting process requires some moisture. The microorganisms that occur naturally in decomposing piles and break down the contents can become dehydrated, falter, and die. On the other hand, if an overzealous hose or heavy rains drench the pile, the microorganisms drown. Your best bet is to keep it slightly damp, as moist as a well-wrung sponge. Check on the pile occasionally. If it appears dry, sprinkle it or poke some holes here and there and run hose water in for a few minutes. Covering the pile helps maintain an even moisture level.

Over time, a good layered compost pile can become compacted, and decomposition will slow down. Stirring it occasionally keeps it aerated, giving those all-important microorganisms the oxygen they need to do their work. Just poke in a pole, branch, or shovel handle and wiggle it. Or use a garden fork to give the pile a good healthy stir.

Warmth encourages active breakdown. While it's true that compost heat is a by-product of intense microbial activity, a spot in the sun is also a good idea. Store-bought composters (even those made of warmth-attracting black plastic) or loose wire- or wood-frame-contained piles set up in shade tend to operate more slowly.

IF I GOOFED, CAN I FIX IT? Compost, and the microorganisms that facilitate breakdown, is forgiving. If your pile is dried out, moisten it. If it's compacted, give it a stir. If it's sitting under shady trees not doing much, move it.

CONTAINERS

AVOID POTTED-PLANT PITFALLS AND GET GREAT DISPLAYS.

Letting plants get too dry

In some places, especially hot, windy, sunny locations, plants in containers can suck up all the available moisture in their potting soil and start to wilt in a single day, or even in a matter of hours. If another day (or two) passes, you may not be able to revive a display.

You might think that plants in containers dry out alarmingly quickly because their root systems aren't huge or able to avail themselves of extensive or deep-ground moisture in hard times, like plants in the garden can. But there's another reason: their root systems are very nearly exposed, as a thin layer of plastic or clay is all that protects them from the elements.

THE RIGHT WAY TO DO IT First, be wary of clay pots, which wick away moisture from roots. Try planting in a slightly smaller plastic pot and nesting it within a clay or ceramic one. Lightly mulching the soil-mix

36

surface has the same benefits as mulching out in the garden proper—
it helps hold in moisture and moderates soil-temperature fluctuations
(you can use a thin layer of bark mulch or even pea gravel). Buy a pot-

ting mix that includes moisture-absorbing coconut hulls, or try
moisture-holding gel or gel beads (follow the label directions or
this material will lead to slimy soil mix).

There are some nifty watering gadgets available, including
gauges that warn you when moisture is getting low by changing
color, and ingenious self-watering pots.

IF I GOOFED, CAN I FIX IT? Bring on the water the moment you notice
a potted plant in distress. If you are lucky and your display is resilient,
the plants will recover. They may shed a few flowers, buds, or leaves,
but will ultimately forgive and generate new ones. Bear in mind,
though, that putting any plant through repeated cycles of drying out
and soaking can be stressful. For most plants, a regular, steady supply
of moisture, with no wilting episodes, is much better for their health
and appearance.

Filling a pot so it's too heavy to move

You have an ambitious plan. You find a big, handsome pot and add a
plant or ensemble of plants, and it looks great. You set up on the patio,
near the hose, or someplace where it's comfortable to do this work
and clean up afterward. Work all finished, you straighten up, admire
the results proudly—and find you can't even lift the creation off the
ground. It may not even be a matter of having a bad back. The display
is simply too heavy.

THE RIGHT WAY TO DO IT Do the work on-site. Take the container to its intended location and spend a few moments making sure it is secure and level and can be viewed from an attractive angle. Only then should you fill it. Granted, doing the project this way can be inconvenient. The spot might be far from a water source, and you need to soak the creation well not only on planting day, but regularly thereafter. Tote along a watering can. The soil mix, drainage stones, and potted plants you mean to transplant into the display can make a mess as you put it all together. Bring a tarp, which you can gather up when you're done, drag away, and shake or hose off as needed.

IF I GOOFED, CAN I FIX IT? The worst-case scenario is undoing all your work and starting over. Easier possible solutions include moving the unwieldy container with a few strong helpers, using a dolly, or maneuvering the plant onto a board or tarp and dragging it to its destination.

Using a large container for a small plant

It seems like a savvy gardening tactic to put a small plant into a large pot, windowbox, urn, or planter, as you are allowing for future growth. And unlike in the yard, you generally don't have to worry about weeds moving in and crowding out the plant. However, this sensible-sounding plan can and does go awry when the small plant really is a small or slow-growing customer destined never to get very large. The result looks bad because the plant is overwhelmed by its surroundings—a classic example is a dwarf conifer plunked into a half-barrel container. Additionally, a small plant can dry out quickly, as water has to disperse throughout the entire pot.

THE RIGHT WAY TO DO IT Whenever you are pairing a plant and a container, aim for compatible size. A small pot-grown plant doesn't have to contend with competition from weeds or encroachment by garden plants, so it should be free to reach mature size. The key is knowing what that size is going to be.

A widely acknowledged design principle is to keep the ultimate plant-to-pot ratio at about 1:1. Put that cute dwarf conifer in a smaller container that will accommodate its root system but also be a fair and even match for its height and girth.

IF I GOOFED, CAN I FIX IT? Transplant the little plant into a smaller home. You can do this at almost any time, even in the heat of summer, if after the move you pamper the plant with a bit of sheltering shade and plenty of water until it settles in, at which time you can return it to the intended spot and adjust its care as needed.

Alternatively, you can add some supporting-player plants to the container. If you wish to retain your original vision of it being the star of the pot, just add shorter or sprawling plants around it. If your star has flowers, choose foliage plants.

Using a container without a drainage hole

It's a sad fact that some attractive or appealing containers lack drainage holes in the bottom to let out excess water. This is true of fun found containers, like vintage teapots, but it is unfortunately a common problem even with pots clearly being sold for planting (what were they thinking?). If excess water cannot get out of the bottom, sogginess results. Roots are deprived of oxygen and will rot.

THE RIGHT WAY TO DO IT You don't have to forgo the beautiful ceramic pot or the charming kettle as a home for a plant display; you just have to be sure drainage is provided for. It may be possible to poke or drill holes in the bottom, depending on what the item is made of and whether you have a tool that can do this (note that drilling holes in a flat-bottomed clay pot can lead to the container breaking into pieces). If you can't create holes, there are two other solutions.

First, try nesting a somewhat smaller plastic pot with drainage holes inside the larger decorative pot. Take care not to overwater, as excess will drain into the larger container and create standing water. Alternatively, line the bottom of an undrained container with a layer of small rocks or pebbles (some gardeners use Styrofoam packing peanuts, but these break down eventually). This creates an area where excess water can flow and, hopefully, wick back up into the soil mix above as needed. A drainage layer helps prevent the plants in the pot from experiencing incessant wet feet; that is, drowning in standing water or drenched mix. This tack is not ideal, but certainly it's better than no drainage provision.

IF I GOOFED, CAN I FIX IT? Yes. Carefully remove the plant or plants and cover the root system(s) with a damp cloth to prevent them from drying out while you work. Scoop out all the soil mix and rinse out the container. At this point, you can either poke or drill drainage holes in the bottom or line the bottom. Return the soil mix to the pot, replant, and water.

DESIGN

FOR BETTER RESULTS, UNDERSTAND AND USE TRIED-AND-TRUE BASICS.

42

Planting too many singletons

Buying only one individual of a plant because you like it is not just a rookie blunder—seasoned plant collectors succumb to this temptation all the time. Assuming you can make the plant happy (enough sun, the right soil, and so on), you may find that even if well grown, the solo performer looks isolated or awkward, or gets dominated by larger or flashier plants growing nearby. The bigger the garden or flowerbed, the more easily the beloved singleton seems to get lost in the shuffle. This turn of events takes some of the pleasure out of enjoying your acquisition or showing it off to garden visitors.

THE RIGHT WAY TO DO IT Drifts of color provided by grouping several or many individuals of a certain plant is a tried-and-true garden-design concept. Indeed, it is naturally pleasing to the eye, borrowed from the way like plants congregate in meadows or along roadsides.

Drifts also unify a garden, giving it a balanced beauty that satisfies viewers. If you really like a plant and want to show off its best features, repetition works. Buy plenty, plant plenty. (This has another practical benefit: it hedges your bets in case one or two individuals do poorly or die.) If your garden isn't very big or you are a plant collector at heart, resolve this problem and protect your garden's diversity by planting in small clumps of three, five, or seven.

IF I GOOFED, CAN I FIX IT? There are several ways to fix the lost-in-the-crowd problem. Buy more and group as described. Or install attendant plants that flatter your favorite either by matching its flower or foliage color or creating dramatic contrast. Or dig it up and display it in a handsome pot.

Planting without a plan

If you don't think about what you could do, you won't realize a good or attractive garden. Instead, you may buy and plant willy-nilly until the yard looks like a hodgepodge.

THE RIGHT WAY TO DO IT Make a general plan, or a modifiable plan, to develop some sort of overall vision. To jog your thinking, hire a professional landscape designer, thumb through gardening magazines and books for ideas and inspiration, attend garden tours and take pictures and ask questions, poke around on the Internet for hours reading articles and lurking in gardening chat rooms, and take an adult-education class or invest in a do-it-yourself kit (perhaps with a software program to assist you).

44

No matter how intensely or casually you plan your home landscape, it bears thought. Should it match your home's color or architecture? Should it be formal or like a cottage garden? What color theme would you like? Will you include nonplant elements, such as garden furniture, an arbor, a birdbath, or gazing globes? If so, consider how to integrate these with the plants.

When implementing your plan, use accurate information. Know what kind of soil you have (and be prepared to either improve it or install native plants) and understand where the sunny and shady spots are. Be realistic about maintenance—fussy plants, big lawns, and watering demands have been the downfalls of many well-laid plans. If the size of the project overwhelms you or you have time and budget considerations, take on one area or bed at a time.

IF I GOOFED, CAN I FIX IT? Fix a hodgepodge? Bring beauty and style to a lackluster yard? Absolutely. Make a careful plan that includes judiciously removing what you no longer like as you install improvements. Unless you have lots of time, money, and energy, the new, improved garden will not happen quickly, and razing what exists could be exhausting and might invite weeds. Cut yourself some slack—become a savvy garden designer gradually.

Planting too many things that bloom at the same time

You want a garden bursting with color, so you head to the garden center on a nice spring day to buy all sorts of plants. You were smart enough to choose annuals on the verge of blooming, hinting at the glorious show that soon appears in your yard. If you selected perennials, you picked ones that were in bloom or looked like color was on the way.

The peak passes, flowering slows down or stops—and it's a letdown. Looking back, you're disappointed. You wonder if anything blooms well later in summer or in the fall, and how to make a longer-lasting show.

THE RIGHT WAY TO DO IT While it's true that many popular plants, annuals and perennials alike, bloom around early summer and then slow  down, you can get an extended show by becoming a more educated shopper. Impulse buying is not the way to go. Make a list ahead of time, just like you do when you buy groceries with a special recipe in mind.

Information about bloom seasons is widely available. Group your wish list into late spring, early summer, midsummer, and late summer into fall. Make a separate listing of plants that bloom over an extended period to form the backbone of your colorful flower garden. Then shop from your list. (Your garden center may not organize its offerings in this way—many don't.) When you get your plants home, be sure to give them appropriate spots and good care so they can realize your vision of a long-blooming, colorful garden.

IF I GOOFED, CAN I FIX IT? Yes. You can remove plants and replace them with later bloomers or other colors. You can shift around others. Do your homework on those that bloom at other times, and add plants as you find them. Remember, however, that annuals and perennials fare better when planted in cooler weather. Making additions or changes during the heat of summer is hard on plants.

46

Planting a tall plant so it blocks a shorter one

Here's a problem you don't always notice until it's too late. Midway through the summer, the verbascum is suddenly towering in front of the irises or petunias and they are lost to view, and the flowerbed just looks wrong. Perhaps when you bought the plant as a tidy rosette, you didn't quite realize what big flower stalks it was capable of making. Maybe you simply didn't check expected mature heights of the plants before you placed them. In any event, you now have a design problem, and you are reluctant to restore ordering by chopping down a blooming plant in its prime.

THE RIGHT WAY TO DO IT Flowerbed planning is not difficult, nor do you have to start with a clean slate. Just make sure you know about a plant's growth habit, bloom season, and expected mature height. If this information is not on the nursery tag, or some of it is missing, do some research. This data is available anywhere from plant catalogs to web searches to gardening books.

The general rule is to relegate the tallest plants to the back of a bed, medium-height ones to the middle, and short and sprawling ones to the front (or if the bed is an island, tall in the center, and so forth). Even those of us with rebellious personalities have to concede that a display that applies this principle looks good. Depending on how much space you have to work with, there can be some flexibility. Yes, there are exceptions; for example, you can place a tall, airy Japanese anemone in front of some hostas and you'll still be able to view them through it.

IF I GOOFED, CAN I FIX IT? You can move a too-tall plant to a more suitable backdrop after it is done blooming. Or you can groom it judiciously so it doesn't totally obscure the plants behind it. If a tall plant is flopping over its neighbors, stake it, which can have the added benefit of reining in a rangy or too-wide profile.

FERTILIZING

DECODE THE MYSTERIES OF PLANT FOOD SO YOUR PLANTS CAN THRIVE.

Burning plants with fresh manure

It's hard to resist free or cheap fertilizer or compost, and an all-natural product may also appeal to you. Farmers sometimes erect signs advertising free manure, and you are lightening their load if you take some home.

Assuming the manure is from vegetarian animals—cows, sheep, horses, bison, or chickens—it is probably fine to use in your yard and garden. However, if it is fairly fresh, hot, or quite sticky and stinky, it is definitely not ready to use. Shoveling fresh manure onto a garden can have the opposite effect of feeding the soil and plants and improving soil texture. Fresh manure is nitrogen-heavy and will literally fry your plants. You'll see the damage—scorched, wilted plants—quickly and know you did something wrong.

THE RIGHT WAY TO DO IT Let fresh manure sit so it can decompose. Shovel it into an out-of-the-way corner for a season or so. Or add it to your compost pile (but not all at once—layering remains important). Once it has dried out somewhat and is not as smelly, and you can squeeze a handful and appreciate its rich, crumbly texture, it is okay to dig it into your vegetable or flower garden, sprinkle it lightly on the lawn or over the groundcovers, or include it in homemade soil mixes.

IF I GOOFED, CAN I FIX IT? If you realize your blunder pretty quickly, grab a shovel and remove as much of the hot manure as possible. Then let it sit and plan to return it to the garden later. If a delivery of hot manure has already damaged or killed your garden plants, it's not a total loss. You can cart away the hot manure and its victims to your compost pile or a backyard corner and, again, let everything sit and break down for a while before pressing it back into service.

Using the wrong type of fertilizer

Fertilizers are not created equal, and deploying the wrong kind can have consequences. Sprinkling something meant for lawns on your vegetable garden can be destructive because these products often include weedkiller, which will harm unintended targets. Also, your soil can wind up with excessive levels of phosphorus and potassium, which can damage plants and adversely affect beneficial soil microorganisms.

It helps to know what kind of N-P-K formulation you're using. (N = nitrogen, P = phosphorus, and K = potassium; these are the major elements plants need to prosper, and their relative proportion is

always listed on the fertilizer package.) Specialized fertilizers can have strange imbalances. Bonemeal, popular for bulb plantings, has no potassium and plentiful phosphorus (2.5-24-0). Wood ashes, which some gardeners have in abundance, contain no nitrogen at all (0-2-5). Plants that are given the wrong food react in different ways. For example, excess nitrogen prevents eggplants from flowering and causes carrots to fork. Other plants may simply shrivel, grow slowly, or sulk. Not what you had in mind.

THE RIGHT WAY TO DO IT Plants generally need more nitrogen than the other two, so it's best to look for a formulation with an N-P-K ratio of 5-1-2 or 5-1-3. This is preferable to fertilizers in which the ratio numbers are the same for all three elements (such as 10-10-10).

If you'd rather use natural or organic fertilizers, dried cow manure (approximately 2-1.5-2) and fish meal (usually 9-7-3) are good bets. And many perennials and woody plants need no fertilizer other than good, homemade compost. If you are growing plants that need or would benefit from a specialized fertilizer, research what type or formulation to use, how much, and when.

IF I GOOFED, CAN I FIX IT? Hopefully you realized your error after only one episode. If you did not feed with a heavy hand, chances are the plants will forgive and forget. However, if they are damaged or they die, learn your lesson. Don't do it again.

Feeding plants at the wrong time of year

Feeding your plants is generally a good idea, particularly if you are trying to coax maximum performance, such as lots of blooms or robust growth, in their early years. What the plant-food label may not emphasize, or you might overlook, is that it is meant to be used on actively growing plants. If you fertilize perennials or flowering shrubs in the fall, you'll spur the plants to generate fresh new growth just as they should be slowing down for the year. And that growth is tender and vulnerable to cold weather, so your good intentions might lead to the plants being harmed.

THE RIGHT WAY TO DO IT Apply plant food only to plants in active growth in spring, summer, and maybe late summer. Wind down and stop as fall approaches. Plants should head into winter hale and healthy, but not bursting with energy or fresh new growth, or jacked up on fertilizer. Also, be sure to match the fertilizer to the plant, and to follow the dosage, application, and frequency information on the product label. Finally, it is always a good idea to apply plant food to damp ground and to water it in well afterward. This ensures the food reaches the root system and gets taken up to benefit the growing plant.

IF I GOOFED, CAN I FIX IT? If you realize your error within a day or so of dosing the plants, water the area thoroughly to dilute or rinse away the fertilizer. If you realize your error too late—for example, you start seeing new buds and a killing frost is predicted—take steps to minimize damage. Cover the plants with old sheets, blankets, or upended cardboard boxes for the night.

FRUITS AND FRUIT TREES

FROM SHOPPING TO CARE, LEARN THE KEYS TO A DELICIOUS HOMEGROWN HARVEST.

54

Choosing fruit-tree varieties that get too big

When you decide to grow your own tree fruit, you eagerly look forward to the delicious homegrown harvest. But if you pick a variety based solely on flavor, color, or appearance, you could be making a mistake. The ones you have relished at roadside stands, farmers' markets, or the grocery store may be fine candidates for an orchard but too big for the average yard. You may be willing to pamper the tree and wait a few years for a harvest, but you might not be prepared for the height and spread. And by the time you realize your sweet little tree has matured into a robust plant that is bumping against the house, garage, fence, or overhead wires, you may be reluctant to rein in its growth.

THE RIGHT WAY TO DO IT Don't go by the size of the tree at the time of purchase and planting. Fruit trees of all sizes are almost always sold as one- or two-year-old plants, and initial size does not indicate how big they will become at bearing age. The nursery should provide this information; if it's not on the tag, ask.

Your best bet may be a dwarf or semidwarf variety—normal-size fruit on a smaller tree. Also, find out if your tree is grafted; that is, whether the desired fruit variety has been attached to a dwarfing rootstock. If it has, take care when planting so you do not bury the bud union (the graft bulge), or the scion (the main part of the tree that is grafted atop the rootstock) might take it upon itself to root, spoiling the tree's dwarf habit.

IF I GOOFED, CAN I FIX IT? If you've had the tree for a few years, you probably don't want to cut it down and start over. Nor will it be easy to move it to an area with more elbow room. Realize that even if dramatic pruning is needed, you will harm the tree if you try to accomplish it in one season. Instead, formulate a pruning-back program of several years. Work when the tree is dormant, in early spring, and aim to retain a structurally sound form by shortening long limbs and removing crowded branches.

Not providing a pollinator tree

You may be enchanted and hopeful when your lone fruit tree sports a flurry of flowers in spring. But if fruits do not set after the petals fall, your delight may turn to frustration or bafflement. Your solo tree might lack a pollinator.

56

Apples and pears, most sweet cherries, and some other fruits will not set fruit if their flowers are only self-pollinated. A pollinator—another similar tree that blooms at about the same time—is needed to provide a separate pollen source. Only then will fruit form.

THE RIGHT WAY TO DO IT Find out if a backyard fruit tree needs a pollinator when you buy it. Not only should the nursery disclose this important information, but it should offer such trees in pairs. They need not be exactly the same variety, just ones that bloom at about the same time. Alternatively, you might be fortunate to have a neighbor with a similar fruit tree. However, this cheat will work only if that tree is within about 100 feet of yours.

IF I GOOFED, CAN I FIX IT? The only way to help a lone apple or pear tree get pollinated is to provide a pollinator. Get another tree and plant it close to the first one. If your space is really limited, consider replacing it. There are a number of self-pollinating, self-fruitful tree varieties, including peaches, nectarines, some plums, and some cherries.

WHAT ELSE?

There are other reasons fruit trees don't bear fruit. Sometimes they are just too young—certain varieties can take five to seven years before producing their first good crop. Or perhaps a very cold winter or a late-spring frost killed the flower buds or flowers, or a rainy spring prevented bees from doing their pollination work. Or the tree may be in poor health, diseased, or riddled with insect pests.

Failing to protect fruit crops from wildlife

Your great excitement at seeing a bounty of fruit growing in your yard can be dashed quickly if you fail to protect the crop. Birds especially love fresh fruit and can swoop in overnight, it seems, to strip your berry bushes or strawberry beds. Birds may peck and ruin fruit on trees, as well. And sometimes bigger animals—including, but not limited to, porcupines—can raid fruit trees, such as apple. This state of affairs is at best annoying (if the pests don't get everything) and at worst maddening (if they eat or damage most of your crop).

THE RIGHT WAY TO DO IT It's not hard to protect ripening fruit. You can throw something, like light netting, over the plant to discourage the birds but still allow in light and air. If you have more than a few bushes or your strawberry bed is large, rig a support with wooden stakes and

58

drape the protective netting over that, tacking it in place here and there so it doesn't blow loose. Netting is also available for draping over fruit trees, although if yours are tall, getting it on and off can be tricky. Other deterrents to try include: attaching fluttering flash (reflective) tape to or close to the fruit plants and setting up scarecrows, fake owls, fake snakes, motion-detector water sprayers, or a prowling outdoor cat or two (try setting the cat food under the trees, but remove this bait if other creatures appear to partake). And don't worry about whether any of this makes your plants and yard look cluttered or unattractive. It's only temporary. This is war.

IF I GOOFED, CAN I FIX IT? No, but there's always next year. Plan to protect your fruit, and to make your move early in the ripening season. If you're not sure what works best, experiment or deploy a variety of tactics.

Leaving fruit trees vulnerable to animal damage

With hope and anticipation, you planted a young fruit tree this spring or summer and have been taking good care of it. When winter comes, it goes dormant. You diligently mulch around the base to add a layer of protection for the root system. Spring returns, and you are disappointed to find that the tree does not seem to be coming back to life. It appears dead, or nearly so.

What happened? Close inspection reveals that the slender trunk has been nibbled. A lot. A young fruit tree may or may not be able to recover from chewing damage inflicted by rodents (such as mice) and rabbits over the winter months.

THE RIGHT WAY TO DO IT In colder climates, it's a good idea to spread winter mulch around a fruit tree that is still getting established. However, a thick layer is just an invitation to small rodents to nest conveniently close to a winter food source.

The best way to shield young fruit trees is to securely wrap a cylinder of wire netting or hardware cloth around the trunk in autumn. It should be a few inches out and pushed into the ground a ways, for stability as well as to discourage any tunneling marauders. You can remove both mulch and shield when spring returns. The critters will have plenty of other good things to eat by then.

IF I GOOFED, CAN I FIX IT? Arborists say that a tree that is two-thirds (or more) girdled—that is, has missing or damaged outer bark—is probably fatally wounded. The more slender the tree, the more vulnerable it is. With some pampering, you may be able to bring your tree back from the brink. Certainly watch it throughout spring for signs of life and returning health. If it simply doesn't recover, you will have to cut it down and start over with a new one, which you will protect well.

GARDEN CONDITIONS

WORK WITH, NOT AGAINST, YOUR YARD'S ASSETS AND REALITIES.

Not knowing your hardiness zone

Nobody mentioned hardiness zones when you went shopping. You picked up some plants from a local nursery, or selected them from catalogs or websites, gathering those you liked and thought would look pretty in your yard. You planted them. One cold winter or blazing summer later, some of these purchases are dead.

Not all plants do well everywhere. But if you planted properly and took good care of a new plant and it still died, it's possible you made the wrong choice for your zone.

THE RIGHT WAY TO DO IT First, decide which zone map makes the most sense for where you live. There are three. The most widely used is the USDA Plant Hardiness Zone Map. North America has been mapped into climatic regions according to each one's average minimum temperature annually. The very coldest zone is 1, and the hottest is 11. If you live in Zone 6 and try a plant rated only to Zone 8, it will likely die over the winter. For temperature ranges by zone, please see "Zone Matters" on page 206.

The Heat Zone Map, created by the American Horticultural Society (AHS), is intended for gardeners in the South and Gulf Coast, where summer heat and drought can dramatically affect plant survival. The 12 zones of this map indicate the average number of days each year that a given region experiences temperatures over 86 degrees Fahrenheit, the temperature at which plants begin to suffer damage. Some regional nurseries and publications refer to these zones. Some gardeners have found the information too limited to be useful. And Sunset, publisher of a popular magazine and books aimed at the West, has a complex map of 24 zones to help those gardeners decide which plants can live in their gardens.

Next, buy only plants rated to survive in your zone. Most do well in a range of zones, such as hardy in Zones 3 to 6. You can take a chance one zone either way, if you wish, but your best bet is to stay within the guideline. Don't know a plant's rating? Ask where you bought it; a reputable nursery will gladly tell you. Or look it up in a reference book or plant catalog, or online.

IF I GOOFED, CAN I FIX IT? A dead plant cannot be revived, but you can learn from your mistakes. You might find acceptable substitutes for the plant you lost. For example, there are red-flowered roses rated for all different zones.

Not knowing how much sunlight your yard gets

The urge to landscape or plant a bountiful garden is hard to resist. Sometimes you can dash off down that trail only to find, after a few weeks or just one season, that something is not right. Even though you chose healthy plants, planted them properly in good or improved soil, and took good care of them, they are not doing well. It's a frustrating, dismaying situation.

You may have made a very basic goof. You planted shade plants in sun (which causes their leaves to bleach out and flowering to falter) or sun plants in shade (growth is poor or lanky, and there are few flowers). Many popular plants simply do not tolerate a wide range of exposures, particularly when they are just starting out. Put in an inappropriate spot, they will not thrive.

THE RIGHT WAY TO DO IT Landscape smart. Do your homework before you add a single new plant. Begin by assessing the light conditions in your yard at different times of the day, not just when you are usually at home or in the yard, and in different seasons. A spot that is in full sun in summer could easily be in shade in the fall, as shorter days cast the longest shadows.

If, for example, you wish to grow sun-loving plants (flowers, a vegetable garden), determine what time of day yields the most sunlight in what spots. In more temperate climates, a location with several hours of full-on, or nearly full-on, sun in the middle of the day would be good. In areas with really blazing summers, a location that gets a little shade relief from a tree or two, or the shadow of your house, is advisable.

IF I GOOFED, CAN I FIX IT? Yes. You can move a plant to a more appropriate spot, preferably in less stressful times, such as spring or fall. You can cut down a tree that is shading an area too much, or at least remove some of its lower limbs. Or you can get plants that are a good match for the existing conditions.

Not taking advantage of microclimates

There are more complicated definitions that take into account elevation and temperature ranges, but the simplest is that a microclimate is a location in your home landscape that has unique conditions. It could be a slope or embankment, a low and boggy area, or a spot constantly shaded by your house, garage, or a fence. When you attempt to garden in such a spot without taking into account its conditions, your scheme may fail, plants may struggle or die, and the results won't be what you expected.

THE RIGHT WAY TO DO IT Walk around your property to determine if
you have microclimate areas. Look for spots that are different from the
main areas. Once you identify a microclimate area, learn more about
it. For example, a north-facing slope will be colder than a south-facing
one. The area at the base of the slope will make a cold pocket because
chilly air flows downhill. Colder air and less sun mean plants will start
to grow and come into bloom more slowly in spring, but they will be
less vulnerable to late frosts. A spot shaded by structures or trees will
also have such qualities, but plants that need some relief from hot
summer sun may do better there. Dry soil and perpetually wet soil can
also affect growth and cold-hardiness.

Wherever possible, turn a microclimate area's conditions into an ad-
vantage. More tender plants that could be damaged by late frosts, for
example, might prosper if you plant them on the north-facing slope. If
a spot is soggy and shady, rather than draining it, filling it in, or cutting
down encroaching trees, consider seeking out and installing plants that
like such conditions.

IF I GOOFED, CAN I FIX IT? If you've made a terrible match, such as putting a sun-loving, drought-tolerant perennial in a shady, damp spot,
move it while it's still alive. Hopefully it can have a good new home
elsewhere in your yard.

If a match is iffy, keep an eye on the plant and the site and decide
who you want to win. You can reduce shade and change the microclimate by pruning or removing overhanging trees, or you may decide to
relandscape the area more appropriately.

THE GARDENER'S HEALTH AND SAFETY

IT'S IMPORTANT TO TAKE CARE OF YOURSELF WHILE TAKING CARE OF YOUR GARDEN.

Failing to protect your skin while working outdoors

In good weather, a quick nip into the yard often blossoms into a major gardening project. If you are not properly prepared, you may stumble indoors a few hours later sunburned and bug-bitten. Sure, the dirt and sweat will wash off, but the miserable consequences of not protecting yourself will last longer—and can take the joy right out of gardening.

It's not just coping with sunburn in places you aren't used to shielding, like the tops of your ears or your lower back, or itchy mosquito bites. Beyond the discomfort is the risk of dehydration, allergic reactions, heat exhaustion, and even skin cancer.

THE RIGHT WAY TO DO IT Harming or depleting yourself is totally avoidable. Wide-brimmed hats are great not only for protecting your head and neck from excessive sun exposure, but also for keeping little flies and gnats at bay (they don't seem to want to travel under the brim). Even so, do not forget sunscreen. Apply it indoors, well before you get hot and sweaty, and replenish every now and then on a long day. Higher SPF numbers provide better protection, so choose a product labeled 30 or 45.

A bandanna can be used instead of or with a hat, and if the day is quite hot, you can soak it in cool water, wring it out, and tie it around your head or neck. As for bug spray, choose one that works for you, but be aware that it can sweat away. Be sure to reapply. Finally, bring along a bottle of water and take regular sips.

IF I GOOFED, CAN I FIX IT? If you went out without sunscreen and insect repellent, and didn't shield your head and neck, have the self-discipline to double back and cover yourself. If it helps you remember, put up hooks or set out a basket or box with what you need in a convenient spot, such as near the back door or close to your gardening tools.

Doing tasks that could injure you

Some garden projects are obviously risky, like removing limbs or taking down a tree with a chainsaw. And others look doable or easy but turn out to be difficult and perhaps even dangerous, such as maneuvering a large pot or trying to crowbar a big rock out of the ground.

Gardeners can be driven or obsessive, and we are also natural do-it-yourselfers, which means we sometimes do hazardous or stupid things. A trip to the emergency room to deal with a gash, a poked-eye injury, or a badly strained back is only a symptom of what we do to ourselves.

The real problem is misjudging our abilities, our equipment, and the plant or project at hand.

THE RIGHT WAY TO DO IT Get a second opinion before starting. Ask a family member, a neighbor, another gardener, or a professional arborist for an opinion on your project and your planned approach. This may persuade you to take another tack, call your attention to some risk you overlooked or underestimated, or convince you to call in help. If it appears you don't have the strength, the right tools, or a safe and sensible approach, adjust your plans accordingly.

IF I GOOFED, CAN I FIX IT? Keep your priorities straight. If you hurt yourself, or think you might have, stop. Forget about the tree, the stump, the pot, or the rock. Assess, ask for help, get medical treatment—whatever is required.

As for the project that led to your injury, hopefully you can safely abandon it. If you're leaving a limb hanging or you have created another hazard, block off the area or get someone else to worry about it. Take care of yourself first.

Not wearing protective gear

When you forget to use goggles to protect your eyes from flying debris or don't wear muffs to shield your ears from the din of loud tools—perhaps the two most common garden-work hazards—you will almost certainly get hurt. Protecting your fingers, hands, and arms is important when you work with sharp pruning or cutting tools, thorny or prickly plants, or plants that cause rashes (such as poison ivy and poison oak). You should also don long, heavy pants and durable shoes (not only to protect your feet but for safe, secure footing).

THE RIGHT WAY TO DO IT Get protective wear together before you need it. Gather everything you might ever need, from goggles to appropriate clothing, and put it all in one place. Suit up before stepping outside. It is better to overcover yourself than to leave yourself exposed. When you're done chopping back the bramble bushes or pruning the trees, return everything to the staging area, unless it needs to be laundered first. If you make this a habit, you will never regret it. There is the argument that suiting up may make you overconfident, such as the person who dons heavy leather chaps while using a chainsaw and then lets the saw harmlessly swipe the pants while working. Another possible problem is wearing too-heavy gloves that compromise your grip on a tool. The answer is to have a prudent respect for protecting your life and limbs and for the potential hazards of the work.

IF I GOOFED, CAN I FIX IT? It's too late if you cut or otherwise hurt yourself, or got poison ivy. After you treat the problem and recover, all you can do is change your ways and work more safely in the future. While you're at it, you might share the story of your mishap with others so that they, too, learn from your mistake.

Trying to do professional-level projects

There are certain garden projects that, while daunting, you think you can do yourself. Perhaps you are trying to save money, but you are

unlikely to save time if you take on something you have never done before.

Tasks that fall into this category include: removing a stump, taking down a big tree or a hazardous overhanging branch, installing a water garden, building a big garden structure such as a pergola or gazebo, laying out a flagstone or brick walkway, and putting in a new lawn.

This is not to say that determined, fit, well-equipped, pragmatic, and careful gardeners can't teach themselves to do such projects and succeed. But you should not take on something you don't feel confident about. You risk wasting your money and your time. You might damage your yard or home, or hurt yourself or someone else.

THE RIGHT WAY TO DO IT Before you begin a big garden project or fix, ask: Can I really do this myself? Do I have the strength and resources, the time, enough money for the necessary supplies, the right tools, the patience? If friends or family are doubtful, maybe you need to listen to them.

If you are mainly trying to save money, consider asking a professional to discuss the project. He may charge a small site-visit fee, but his input will be worth it. You might propose a hybrid approach: maybe he starts the project and you finish it; you launch it and he completes it; or he allows you to work alongside him.

IF I GOOFED, CAN I FIX IT? It's humbling to call in professional help after you have messed up a project, but you will have to put aside your pride. Be candid about what you did and did not do; she has to be fully informed if she's going to rescue or redo the project.

Creating hazards

Sometimes you can get so wrapped up in, say, clearing out a new area that you don't notice you've tossed all the rocks or brush right into a pathway or created a gaping hole—short-term hazards for yourself or anyone checking on your progress. Sometimes the effects of yard mistakes aren't immediately apparent, such as when you pull all the plants and weeds out of a slope and the next big rain brings a mudslide. Then there are more ordinary mishaps and dangers, like messing up drainage, stirring hornets' nests, poking your eye on that new green-camouflage stake in the flowerbed, and leaving the hoe on the ground for someone to step on and get a whack in the head.

The common denominator is yardwork carelessness. Sometimes you can get away with it, and then there are the memorable times when you harm yourself, someone else, or a feature or plant in the garden.

THE RIGHT WAY TO DO IT Avoid gardening when you are exhausted, distracted, or rushed, or have poor light. If you have a bigger project in mind, gather information about how to do it, think it through, and work carefully and neatly. It sounds like common sense, but sometimes gardeners get carried away in the heat of the moment. Remember that gardening is a joy when you work steadily and mindfully.

IF I GOOFED, CAN I FIX IT? The fix may not be so much in the corrective action, such as finding a way to stabilize the slope you allowed to erode. Instead, it may be more in your habits—learning to do the corrective work, or the tidying up, deliberately and thoroughly. The root problem was carelessness; the cure is to learn the valuable habit of being careful. It's smarter, safer, and, in the end, more enjoyable.

HERBS

RAISE HEALTHY, RECIPE-BOOSTING FAVORITES.

Harvesting or preserving herbs the wrong way

For most of us, the motivation for growing herbs is not their beauty (although some are quite attractive) but because we want to use them in cooking, homemade vinegars, or teas. The freshness should yield wonderful flavor, but if you harvest an herb too early or too late, or don't treat or preserve the harvest correctly, the flavor is downright disappointing.

THE RIGHT WAY TO DO IT Educate yourself about each herb you grow. Make sure you give it the best possible spot and good care to maximize flavor. Then find out how and when to harvest each one—timing and methods vary considerably, and it is always easier to follow good information and advice than to learn the hard way. For example, for peak flavor, cut basil after flower buds have formed but before they open. Cilantro leaves are tastiest when harvested while small. Grate horseradish roots while still fresh and crisp, as dried ones are lackluster. For basil as well as many other favorite herbs, fresh leaves have the best aroma and strongest flavor. There are exceptions, though, such as sage leaves, which intensify in flavor when dried.

Learn about herb seeds, too, if you're interested in using them. You need to time the harvesting correctly, usually when they are ripe and flavor is good but before they shatter off the plant of their own accord.

Harvested herbs need to be stored properly, which in most cases means in a cool, dry place, in an airtight jar or bag. They may look cute on the kitchen windowsill, but sunlight will bleach the color and flavor right out of them. Leaves put away damp grow moldy, so follow drying instructions with care.

IF I GOOFED, CAN I FIX IT? If you harvested an herb at the wrong time or it lost flavor in storage, you can probably use it safely in a soup or stew. (Rotten or moldy leaves and seeds should not be ingested.) Otherwise, toss the disappointing or failed project in the compost pile and try again next year.

Assuming all herbs like it hot and dry

If you are new to herb gardening, you may assume that common herb plants want a hot, sunny, dryish location. You've seen such herb gardens in enchanting public-garden knot garden displays, in water-conscious-gardening booths at home-and-garden shows, or even in someone else's yard.

You may have also discerned that many herbs are fairly easy to grow and are low maintenance. And so, based on these assumptions, you confidently plant an assortment—say, oregano, thyme, basil, mint, sage, and parsley. Some do well, while others do not. After a while, as you view your herb patch or harvest with a twinge of disappointment, you suspect there is something you don't know, or that you made a wrong assumption.

 **THE RIGHT WAY TO DO IT** Always do a little homework before buying and planting herbs. Cultural requirements are easily found online, in gardening books and catalogs, and on the small tag wedged into the pot at the nursery. Many herbs prefer sunny spots with well-drained soil (oregano, thyme, and sage, certainly), but others do not (mint likes damp ground and a bit of shade, and parsley and basil prosper in moderately rich, moist, well-drained soil). You can still enjoy an herb area or herb garden if you group together plants with similar preferences.

Despite their sometimes informal or even weedy appearance, herbs require care. Treat them as well as you do any other garden citizen: plant them in an appropriate spot, and groom and water them regularly. As a general rule, most herbs do not require fertilizing or a great deal of pampering, but neither do they thrive on neglect.

IF I GOOFED, CAN I FIX IT? Many herbs are resilient, so moving misplaced plants to a more suitable spot is usually easy and successful. Take good care of them in their new home until they are established, and they should do fine.

Letting mint become a pest

Mint is an easy herb to grow, justly popular for its refreshing contribution to summer salads, fruit medleys, and various drinks. You probably already know that mint likes damp soil. Putting it near the hose (especially if yours is a bit leaky at the point of connection) is a logical move. Mint never seems to require much care, so you don't pay it much attention other than clipping off a few sprigs when you need it in the kitchen.

A happy mint plant can easily become a real garden thug, its vigorous roots spreading quickly until it has invaded nearby flowerbeds and popped up in the lawn. Cutting it back seems to encouragerather than control it, and soon you find that the plant's growth exceeds the amount you will ever need in your recipes, and it has become a real nuisance.

THE RIGHT WAY TO DO IT Control the root growth, and you ought to be able to rein in even the most rampant mint plant. You can simply grow mint in a container, or even a hanging basket, and completely avoid the problem. If you prefer your mint in the ground, plant it in a bottomless pot or can, or surround it with an underground barrier. Either way, deeper is better—some gardeners have found 10 inches down is necessary.

Alternatively, try a less-invasive species. Corsican mint, *Mentha requienii*, is a fine choice. It has a low, ground-covering habit; its only drawback is that it's not as cold-hardy as the more widely available peppermint and spearmint.

IF I GOOFED, CAN I FIX IT? You can eradicate an unwelcome, aggressive mint patch by digging up the entire plant. Cutting back does not work well because it inspires new, thicker growth (the same way pinching back houseplants makes them bushier). Hopefully you can use some of it. If you give away your unwanted mint plants, caution the recipients so they don't inherit your struggles.

LAWNS

SAVE TIME, WATER, AND TROUBLE WHILE TENDING A LUSH GREENSWARD.

Overwatering or wasting water

Figuring out how much to water your lawn—or, more specifically, how long to run the sprinkler—is tricky, to be sure. It can vary with the type of grass or soil, as well as your area's climate and weather. A sure sign your watering is not effective, however, is runoff, when water is rolling down the driveway or onto the sidewalk or otherwise not being absorbed.

Overwatering is harmful. It doesn't just waste water, but also may wash fertilizer into your area's waterways or water table. Overwatering can also erode your soil or damage its structure. The grass in an oversaturated lawn suffers because its roots are deprived of necessary oxygen. A soggy lawn is more vulnerable to diseases, too.

THE RIGHT WAY TO DO IT The general guideline is to apply 1 to 1½ inches of water to an actively growing lawn each week, tweaking this amount to suit your particular conditions and local weather or rainfall. You probably know that most lawn grasses are shallow-rooted, but no matter how deep the roots are, the object is to get water to them. Check by digging after you water: Plunge a trowel down about 6 inches and look, then adjust future waterings accordingly. Remember to let the lawn dry out between waterings, but don't let it get too dry—water just runs off parched ground. To save time and water, you might mow a little less often, as frequently cut, shorter grasses dry out faster. Apply the water slowly so it can soak in.

IF I GOOFED, CAN I FIX IT? Commit to spending one or two sessions to getting a handle on watering. Watch what happens and conduct the trowel test. If you discover the water hasn't soaked in deeply enough but is starting to run off, try watering for 10 or 15 minutes, stopping to allow the water to soak in, checking again after 10 or 15 minutes, and repeating as needed.

Cutting the grass too short

You run the risk of cutting a lawn far too short when you adjust the mower blades too low or you mow too often or overzealously. Scalping the grass may make your greensward look patchy and stress it out, causing it to produce shallower roots and exposing it to heat and drought (let your grass be taller in the middle of summer). If a lawn is stressed, it will be more vulnerable to weed or pest invasions.

You might think that mowing low will make your grass grow more slowly so you won't have to mow as often. Wrong—unless you succeed in killing it.

THE RIGHT WAY TO DO IT The correct mowing height varies depending on the type of lawn grass you have and the season, but generally speaking, 2 or 3 inches is fine and generally looks good. If you're uncertain about the correct mowing height, get advice from a local landscaper or lawn service. If you don't know how to set your mower, get help with that, too—and have the blades sharpened, as dull ones tear at and mash the grass.

How often to mow will vary. Cool-season grasses tend to need more frequent mowings in the shoulder seasons of spring and fall, when they are actively growing. Warm-season grasses grow most vigorously in the heat of summer. Your watering schedule, fertilizing regimen, and amount of rainfall will also affect how quickly your grass grows and how often it needs attention. Keep after it, but don't be fanatical. Mow when the grass gets about a third taller than its recommended growing height. More often is detrimental; less often, it gets difficult to cut.

IF I GOOFED, CAN I FIX IT? Let a scalped, stressed-out lawn rest and recover and grow back. If weeds or pests have invaded, you may need to go after them—get professional advice if you are unsure. Resolve to care for the lawn more temperately and consistently in the future.

84

Fertilizing your lawn the wrong way

Those of us who want a green, lush lawn—and who doesn't?—can make the mistake of fertilizing too much. The results are not good. The overdose of nitrogen (lawn fertilizer is mostly nitrogen) will do one of two unfortunate things. It will cause overly lush growth that draws in hungry lawn pests and opportunistic lawn diseases, or it will leave the lawn burnt; that is, looking scorched. Overfeeding is also bad for the environment, as it runs off into and pollutes groundwater or waterways in your neighborhood.

Underfertilizing your lawn is not advisable either. Over time, grass plants deplete the nutrients inherent in the soil. Unlike, say, your vegetable garden or flowerbeds, you are not going to get in there every year and dig in some organic matter. The lawn starts to go downhill, thinning out and looking less green and less healthy. Weeds, many of which relish infertile ground, will invade.

THE RIGHT WAY TO DO IT Fertilizing a lawn correctly means striking a balance between too much and too little. Lawn food is nitrogen-heavy because nitrogen fuels leaf and stem growth. Common N-P-K formulations include 21-0-0 and 22-3-7. Read the label and you will see that dose recommendations are there in some detail, usually based on treating 1000 square feet of lawn. Use a broadcast spreader meant for this purpose.

The label will also advise how often to feed, but ultimately it's up to you and how plush you want the lawn to look. At a minimum, you should feed your lawn once a year—fall for cool-season grasses; spring for warm-season ones. Additional feedings in the shoulder season are explained on the label. Don't feed when the weather is blazing hot and dry; grass growth naturally slows down then.

One last note: never feed a dry lawn. Wait until after watering or a rainfall, and water after feeding, too, so the food reaches the roots.

IF I GOOFED, CAN I FIX IT? Most neglected and abused lawns can be brought back from the brink with good care, or repaired as needed with reseeding or resodding. Thereafter, resolve to apply just enough fertilizer and to do so properly.

Having a lawn that's too big

Sure signs that your lawn is too big: you seem to be spending too much time mowing, your water bills are high, fertilizing has become a costly chore, and areas are being worn down by persistent foot traffic or other uses. Or you are simply not keeping up and the neglect is attracting weeds, pests, or lawn diseases. Another telltale sign is when you don't have enough space for other planting projects, such as a flowerbed, vegetable garden, fruit patch, or outdoor-living area.

THE RIGHT WAY TO DO IT Make it smaller. Map out or roughly sketch your renovation so you don't do more or less work than you really need to. Consult with a landscape designer on alternate plans if you feel daunted.

Dig up lawn grass in spring or fall, not in the heat of summer; it's easier on you and on replacement plants. Depending on the scope of the project, you may wield a sharp-edged shovel or use a tiller. Lawn grass is shallow rooted and relatively easy to dig up. Wet it down before starting, as dampened root systems are easier to extract. If you work with care and it is in decent condition, you might be able to donate it to someone else's yard. Otherwise, compost torn-up grass.

If you want to convert the area to something low-maintenance, replace the lawn with a groundcover or a hardscape (like a patio or a deck). If you are allotting some of the area for other gardening uses, plan for both the new layout and the new plants (how many, what kinds). Soil improvement—adding organic matter—may be in order to make the ground hospitable for the new residents. Note that it may be necessary to consult local regulations concerning landscaping, particularly in planned communities.

IF I GOOFED, CAN I FIX IT? Decide what you can do now. Many gardeners in your shoes reduce the size of their lawns gradually over a period of several years, as fresh ideas, budget, and time allow.

Choosing the wrong grass variety

This is a potential do-it-yourself error. No reputable lawn service or landscaper should ever install a lawn that is unsuitable for your climate or for the amount of sun or shade in your yard. Whether you seed an entire lawn with the wrong sort of grass, or patch or expand with something that doesn't match or thrive, the blunder comes back to the same thing: you didn't do your homework, and the new grass failed or looks lousy.

THE RIGHT WAY TO DO IT To find a grass that will do well in your yard, inquire at a local lawn service, consult reference books, call your local Cooperative Extension office, nose around your favorite garden center (ask questions, read seed-bag labels), and find out what your neighbors are growing successfully.

You will shortly discover that there are many different kinds of grasses, including mixtures. Don't be daunted—narrowing down is easier than you might think. Start by considering only those appropriate in your climate. Generally speaking, warm-season grasses are suitable for the hotter South and West, while cool-season ones do better in the North and East. (If you live in a borderline area, seek more detailed advice.)

As a rule, most grasses and blends do best in sun. If your yard has some shade, it's possible to grow a decent lawn if you choose something specifically marketed for such conditions. If your yard has a little of both, a blend might be right for you.

88

IF I GOOFED, CAN I FIX IT? Just like other garden plants, certain lawn grasses are meant for certain growing conditions. There's not much you can do to persuade them to thrive when they are in the wrong spot, although you might be able to remove growth-inhibiting shade and bring more sun into the yard by pruning back or cutting down encroaching trees and shrubs.

WHAT ELSE?

Sometimes lawn grass fails because you are not taking good care of it. Regular, consistent watering, fertilizing, and mowing may revive faltering grass.

MAINTENANCE AND CLEANUP

YOUR PLANTS AND GARDEN WILL PROSPER WHEN YOU DO THE RIGHT THING.

90

Removing all your dead fall leaves

Autumn blows in, and all the deciduous trees in your and your neighbors' yards fall to the ground, perhaps even to the point of totally obscuring your lawn, so you rake or get out the leaf blower. After all that hard work, you bag all the leaves and set them at the curb for municipal pickup. Except your town won't pick them up because of a prohibition against yard waste in the local landfill. And now your lawn and garden beds are denuded and exposed to the coming winter, including possible freeze-thaw cycles.

THE RIGHT WAY TO DO IT Don't miss this golden opportunity to use free organic matter in your yard and garden. And don't relegate those fall leaves to some far corner of your yard or donate them to your town's composting facility—at least not all of them.

To turn raked-up leaves into mulch for your garden, chop them up a bit so they don't mat down. You don't need a special machine; just run the lawn mower set on high over a low pile a few times. (And prepare to be amazed at how dramatically this reduces the volume of your leaf piles.) Then sprinkle the resulting debris around the yard, several inches thick, to protect plants from winter cold and to prevent frost heaving (newer plants are most vulnerable).

Alternatively, add them to your compost pile so they can rot and be dug into your garden soil next spring. If this overwhelms your pile, bag the excess (use tall biodegradable paper bags; plastic bags seal out air and water, which aid in the natural decomposition process) or create an out-of-the-way staging area you can access later. Note that unless autumn leaves are left to break down and rot for a while, you run the risk of spreading mulch containing seeds that might sprout in your garden (maple and ash keys, for example, or acorns).

IF I GOOFED, CAN I FIX IT? If all your free mulch is gone, swallow your pride and ask your neighbors for some of theirs, or hurry to the garden center and buy and deploy some bagged mulch.

Not using mulch (or using the wrong kind)

Weeds an ongoing problem? Plants constantly need to be watered? This is what happens when you don't mulch, or don't mulch sufficiently, or neglect to replenish mulch when it wears away in a flowerbed, vegetable garden, or other spot where there is open ground around your plants.

Applying the wrong kind of mulch can also have disappointing or annoying results. For example, you might like the tidy look and nice scent of cocoa hulls, but if your weather is hot and dry, a breeze can blow away this lightweight material, and if your weather is damp, the hulls tend to get matted and moldy. Hay can contain weed seeds, and you may discover that you have created quite a problem when they germinate in and among your desired plants. Bark mulch is great around trees and shrubs, but it's a disaster around a strawberry bed because you cannot rake it off in the spring without damaging the plants. And so on.

THE RIGHT WAY TO DO IT Mulch is supposed to be the gardener's friend by helping your garden look attractive and neat. It also inhibits the growth of weeds by physically thwarting their progress and blocking sunlight. And it conserves soil moisture, so you don't have to water as often.

The trick is to lay down mulch neither too thickly (which can smother plants or invite in critters) nor too thinly (in which case it will not be effective). The standard advice is 2 or 3 inches. Avoid pushing it up directly against a plant's main stem or stems, where it can inhibit growth or attract pests and rot. All you need is a nice carpet on the garden's floor. The kind of mulch you use depends on what is readily available and within your budget, and what looks nice to you.

IF I GOOFED, CAN I FIX IT? It's never too late. Be sure to get rid of the weeds before laying down a couple of inches of the mulch. Don't forget to replenish it occasionally, or at least every spring. As for replacing mulch that didn't work out, you can probably find a place to discard it in a little-used part of your yard or in your compost pile.

Misjudging whether a plant is dead

This question can baffle even a seasoned gardener: Because they are not going to revive, is it okay to remove dead, damaged, or diseased branches on your shrubs and trees at any time, including late fall, the winter months, and early spring? Done right, the process yields a healthier plant with a tidier profile.

But what if you can't tell whether a branch or an entire plant is alive or dead? What if it's just dormant and you chop back something you shouldn't have? Live wood cut back in cold or freezing weather can suffer damage as tissues are exposed to wet weather and low temperatures. Plus, the cuts might inspire a fresh flush of new growth that cannot cope with the coming cold weather and will be frosted or blackened.

THE RIGHT WAY TO DO IT When you are doubtful, wait until spring, or longer, and see if any growth appears. Experience will teach you what live wood looks like. Scrutinize the buds. They may not be actively growing, but any green showing indicates that a branch has life in it. Deadwood is dry, and as a result has a different texture. Bark may be starting to peel off. It may cut or snap right off, or resist or squeak to the teeth of a saw or the blade of a clipper. When you examine a cut stem or branch, notice the pith in the very center; in most live plants it is soft and spongy. In dead growth, it has dried out and sometimes darkened. Dispose of diseased branches—don't leave them at the base of the plant.

IF I GOOFED, CAN I FIX IT? Don't do any further cuts until spring returns. Then prune again with care, taking out all damaged wood—any you may have missed earlier, as well as parts that were your fault. Give the plant a good soaking and perhaps a light dose of fertilizer. In other words, pamper it and hope it accepts your apology.

Letting weeds get out of hand

Seemingly overnight, this oversight can go from "the yard looks so-so" to "oh, no!" Nobody, least of all other gardeners, is going to say that eradicating weeds is easy or fun or quick. But when you neglect this basic chore, your garden plants are the big losers. Weeds are thugs, stealing resources like soil space, nutrients, water, and even sunlight by crowding out desirable plants. Once out of control, they invite further problems by providing a haven for pests (animal as well as insect) and plant diseases. If the weed population is really out of hand and you

attack in a clumsy manner—say, start yanking willy-nilly, or resort to liberally spraying an herbicide—you can harm the very plants you were trying to save.

THE RIGHT WAY TO DO IT For weeds that spread by seeds, attack before they flower and ripen. For those that spread via underground runners, or regenerate from bits of roots, remove all of the plant. If you are not sure which mode your weeds use to reproduce and don't want to study their botany, attack on all fronts. Good, sturdy weeding tools are worth investing in.

Remember that most pesky weeds love open ground, poor soil, and plentiful sun, conditions you may be able to control or alter in order to discourage them. Start fighting weeds early in spring, as soon as the yard is showing signs of life. Pull out baby weeds every time you go outside. In the vegetable garden, keep after them with a sharp hoe. Remember that weeds surrender more easily when the ground is damp. Going forward, keep the weed population down by applying several inches of mulch and replenishing throughout the growing season as needed.

IF I GOOFED, CAN I FIX IT? Get a clearer picture of the scope of the problem by chopping back the weed population. Then go in and pull or dig out individual plants, if practical (remember, it's easier when the ground is damp). If an area is really overrun, consider systemic and preemergent herbicides, but always heed all label cautions and instructions. Protect desirable plants by covering or shielding them or digging them up temporarily or moving them to a better spot.

PERENNIALS

BRING OUT THE BEST IN YOUR LONG-TERM GARDEN INVESTMENTS.

Neglecting to stake or support a plant

Some plants are naturally floppy because of weak stems, or the stems have a hard time supporting the weight of heavy flowers. Examples include delphiniums, peonies, golden marguerite, phlox, crocosmias, and lilies. They grow robustly until, over time, they begin to lean or splay. You may step outside one day to find they have keeled over. A blustery summer storm can also flatten these susceptible plants.

Neglecting to support such plants is not good for their appearance or well-being. They will never again stand upright if you let the problem go on for too long.

THE RIGHT WAY TO DO IT Install support well before it is needed, while a perennial is still small. It's easy to situate it over or adjacent to the

98

plant. Among the items you can press into service are peony hoops, tomato cages, wooden and bamboo sticks (solo or in a network or web of string), and branches left over from pruning woody shrubs.

Pick a stronger support than you think you might need, and drive it deeply into the ground so it will be stable when weight leans on it. To fasten an ever-taller plant to its support, use special inexpensive clips sold for this purpose. Or loop loose twine, soft rags, or even strips of old stockings around the stem and the support to minimize abrasion when the wind blows. (Never use wire and never tie tightly.) Finally, if you prefer to camouflage these things, employ green supports and ties.

IF I GOOFED, CAN I FIX IT? You might be able to truss or shore up a downed perennial, but it will look like an afterthought, which it was. If the blooms are presentable, your best bet might be to clip them at ground level and bring a nice bouquet indoors.

WHAT ELSE?

Hometimes perennials are floppy when they really shouldn't be because of overly rich soil or insufficient sunlight. Adjusting site conditions or moving the plants to a more suitable spot ought to help, and should eliminate the need for support.

Neglecting to water in a newly planted perennial

Bringing home a container-grown perennial from the garden center and getting it in the ground seems like a simple procedure. Find an

 appropriate spot, dig a hole, pop it out of its pot, plunk it in, backfill, and done. Right? Not quite. A perennial planted this way might survive, but more than likely the leaves will soon droop and any buds and petals will fall off. In a matter of a few short days, it can falter and die.

Air pockets in the hole, lack of contact between the root system and the surrounding soil, not enough water—all these add up to an uphill battle for a freshly transplanted perennial. The plant needs and deserves better, depending on the care it received at the nursery and the condition it was in when you bought it.

THE RIGHT WAY TO DO IT Make an ample hole in prepared soil. Set in the plant at the same level at which it was growing in the pot (any deeper and you risk burying the crown). If a plant is potbound, wiggle it out carefully to avoid damage and tease apart the roots a bit (never tug it out by the leaves). Gently backfill all around.

Then water in the plant thoroughly. The water hydrates the roots so they will be encouraged to reach out in their new home. Watering may also cause some settling, so double-check and adjust the plant so the crown is not covered. Mulch to conserve moisture and keep weeds at bay.

Then water the new perennial daily or as needed. Do not let it dry out. It will get its legs under it in a couple of weeks, and then you won't have to pamper it as much.

IF I GOOFED, CAN I FIX IT? Try soaking a slumped perennial. If it revives, groom off any dried-out or damaged parts, and resolve to keep it well-watered going forward. If it's dead, dig it out and compost it, and do a better job next time.

Planting shade plants in sun or sun plants in shade

If you're new to gardening, or even if you buy a plant impulsively based on how attractive it is, it's easy to overlook its exposure preference or requirement. Some nurseries segregate sun plants from shade plants to keep you from making this mistake (and to provide the plants with what they need while still on the premises), but not all do so. Or you may know that the spot you have in mind at home is shady, but gamble on a sun lover or one characterized as "full sun to part shade." Either way, once home the plant tends to do poorly. Sun plants grown in shade get leggy as their stems reach or lean in the direction of the most light, and they fail to bloom, don't bloom very generously, or make uncharacteristically small blooms. Shade plants placed in too much sun experience faded or burnt-edged—browned—foliage, and any flowers tend to look dried out or bleached.

THE RIGHT WAY TO DO IT Shop for your garden based on the light conditions at home. How many slots are available in the sunny areas? How many plants do you think you'll need for the shady spots? Do a little homework in gardening books or magazines, or online, and draw up some wish lists—plants by genus, at least. Once at the nursery, stick to your lists and be flexible on exact species and varieties. Or ask the staff for help in finding good substitutes.

IF I GOOFED, CAN I FIX IT? A perennial that is struggling in the wrong spot is not going to improve this season or over the years. Dig it up and move it to a better location, give it away, or discard it and replace it with something more suitable.

Alternatively, gauge whether it might be possible to improve its life. Prune away encroaching, shading plants to give a sun lover more sun, or provide needed protection from hot sun for a shade lover, either with additional landscaping or with a hardscape item, such as lawn furniture, a trellis, or a big potted plant.

Practicing zonal denial

Zonal denial (a phrase coined by Oregon nurseryman Sean Hogan) is a trap that ensnares many an inexperienced gardener (and some experienced ones, too). It means you've fallen for a plant that is too tender for your climate. You saw it in a British garden, or on a trip to Seattle, or in an article in a magazine, and it was love at first sight. Despite knowing the plant probably wouldn't survive in your garden, you tracked it down, bought it, and planted it with care. Maybe you were hoping you'd have a string of mild winters. Or maybe you thought somehow you'd just beat the odds. But then a normal winter comes and goes, and it's a goner. A sad waste of your time and money.

THE RIGHT WAY TO DO IT The only sure way to overcome zonal denial is to use every ounce of willpower and resist buying a plant that isn't hardy for you. Yes, it's difficult. Ask your local nursery to suggest similar plants, or do some research. Often you'll be able to find a plant that has the qualities you're seeking—bold, tropical-looking foliage, for example—as well as the necessary hardiness for your area. It's a tough lesson to learn, but in the long run it's better to accept the realities of your climate than constantly fight them.

IF I GOOFED, CAN I FIX IT? If your plant is not at all hardy in your zone, you may be able to overwinter it indoors in a pot. Many tender plants can survive in a nonfreezing place with just enough light and water to keep them going. If a plant is borderline hardy, you can take your chances, although mulching it would be wise. If such measures are not practical, you enjoyed a special annual for one season, and you can resolve to be more disciplined next year.

Planting at the wrong season or time of day

When you plant a newly acquired perennial between noon and midafternoon, it is subjected to undue stress, even if you do everything else correctly. Leaves and blooms dry out quickly, and the root system may not even have a chance to take up water. The entire plant may just keel over.

Planting in the wrong season is similarly stressful for a transplant. Midsummer—when, granted, there are bargain prices on leftover perennials—is a poor time. The soil has been warming up for weeks and the sun blazes overhead, and the newcomer simply may not be able to stand up to such double-teamed dehydrating conditions. Late summer may not be much better. And while early fall can be fine, later in the season (again, when nurseries unload excess perennials) is not; the plants can't get established before winter's cold shuts down their growth for the year.

THE RIGHT WAY TO DO IT Plant on a cool morning or late in the day. Water well. Protect newly planted perennials by laying down some mulch at their base, and consider erecting a temporary shield from hot sunshine (place lightweight lawn chairs, crates, or a rig of lumber scraps over the newbies for a couple of days). Better yet, plant on a cloudy, misty, or foggy day, which further reduces the threat of dehydration.

Be wary of off-season bargain plants. If they appear to be in decent health and you cannot resist, and thus must plant at a less-than-ideal time, take pains to pamper them. Ample water is always important, coupled with protection.

IF I GOOFED, CAN I FIX IT? If a newly transplanted perennial has collapsed because of heat stress, bring in more water and a protective cover and hope it revives. If it does, continue to give it extra-good care, as the period of stress will have weakened it. If frost nips a newly transplanted perennial, cut it down to the ground, mulch over the root system, and hope for the best. Maybe it will make it through the winter and send up new growth next spring. If not, you'll know better next time.

Planting a peony too deeply

In order for a peony to bloom, the dormant buds near the top of a peony root (known as eyes) need to be fairly close to the surface of the soil. If they're planted deeper than about 2 inches below the soil level, you'll get lots of leaves but no flowers.

THE RIGHT WAY TO DO IT It's easy—don't plant the root clump too deeply. About 1 to 2 inches deep, from where the eyes appear on the root to the surface of the soil, is ideal. Use a ruler if you're nervous about guessing the depth. The planting hole should be about 8 to 10 inches deep, the soil should have lots of compost or humus in it, and the site should be in full sun.

IF I GOOFED, CAN I FIX IT? Unfortunately, there's no quick remedy. If you want flowers and you suspect that too-deep planting is the culprit, you'll need to dig up the root clump—do this in late summer or early fall—and replant it more shallowly. Be gentle. Use a gardening fork, carefully loosen the soil around the plant, and try to keep the root clump intact when you lift it out. You can also take the opportunity

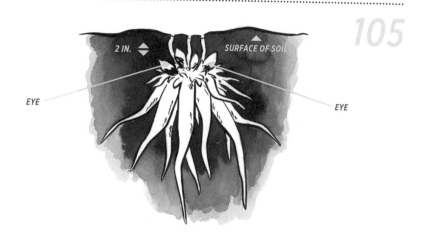

to add compost and organic fertilizer to the planting hole, which will lead to a stronger, lusher plant. If you live in an area that experiences extended subzero temperatures in winter, a light application of organic mulch (shredded bark or leaves) will be beneficial.

WHAT ELSE?

Before you start digging, check to see whether the problem might be too little light—for example, peonies perform poorly if heavily shaded by a tree or other object. If that's the case, you'll need to remove or cut back the source of the shade, or move the peony to a sunnier spot.

Dividing a plant when you shouldn't

Splitting or breaking up mature perennials into smaller plants and replanting the pieces is a great way to get more plants. However, if the piece lacks a sufficient root system, it won't take. If the root system was maimed or dried out during the division process, it won't recover.

If you save the wrong part—keep the old center and discard the smaller, but more vigorous, outer sections—you'll be disappointed. If the piece lacks a growing point (crown), is full of broken shoots, or is pest-infested, the new plant is bound to fail.

THE RIGHT WAY TO DO IT Undertake division or accept divisions only in the spring or fall, when the perennial is not growing at full speed. Spring divisions will soon enjoy a good growing season. Fall divisions can invest some weeks in establishing their root systems before going dormant and then bursting forth the following spring.

Work on a cool, damp day, or at least in the morning or late afternoon, and keep a bucket of water or the hose nearby so you can dampen the roots while they are out of the ground.

Begin by cutting back the foliage and stems to about 6 inches, which is easier to handle. Use a shovel, garden fork, or trowel and work a broad circle around the plant in order to eject most or all of the root system. Break apart the clump into divisions, discarding the older, woody, worn-out center. You may have to pull, tug, tease, or cut apart the pieces, depending on the type of plant and its age. Retain those with a good chunk of growth (or, for daylilies and irises, several fans), with obvious growing points and a hearty clump of roots or rhizomes. Promptly replant divisions in a prepared area, at the same level they were growing before, and water well.

IF I GOOFED, CAN I FIX IT?
Smaller divisions sometimes grow more slowly: don't write them off right away. Dig out and discard pieces that simply aren't viable once you realize your error or if a season in the ground yields no new growth.

PESTS IN YOUR GARDEN

COPE WITH UNWANTED CREATURES IN YOUR YARD AND GARDEN.

108

Turning your garden into a slug motel

Damp yard, especially in the cool evenings and dewy mornings? Shade, too? You have a haven for a most annoying and destructive garden pest: the slug. Slugs feed at night and prefer moist plant material. If you are slow to notice and respond, you will be amazed at how thoroughly they chew up your edible and ornamental plants alike. Favorites include lettuce, spinach, carrot tops, dahlias, marigolds, strawberries, and hostas. At best, the plants will become disfigured and the foliage riddled with nibbled holes or reduced to papery thinness. At worst, the plants will be overrun and will die back.

THE RIGHT WAY TO DO IT Begin by determining how bad the problem is. Do a search-and-destroy mission at night: take a flashlight and a bucket of soapy water for drowning the pests. One or a few nighttime trips may only reduce the population, so traps might be in order. The favored homemade trap is the classic beer in a pie plate; bury it so the rim is slightly above ground level. Or set out an upended, damp clay pot or a cabbage or other large leaf somewhere near the vulnerable plants. Then check and empty the traps each morning.

Store-bought products can also work well. Look for traps that entice the slugs to crawl in and then prevent them from getting out. Baits that contain iron phosphate (like Sluggo) are effective, biodegradable, and environmentally benign.

Barriers are effective when dry, but you'll need to replenish them after a rain. Coarse, scratchy materials to try include: diatomaceous earth, sharp sand, crumbled eggshells, wood ashes, or the ground-up seashells or oyster shells sold for driveways and walkways. Coffee grounds do not work. Place a ring around the base of plants or around the entire bed or garden. Alternatively, try a low fence made of copper barriers, which purportedly administer an unpleasant shock to soft slug bodies.

IF I GOOFED, CAN I FIX IT? If you've lost a lot of plants to slugs, mere traps and barriers may not be your first line of attack. Take a fresh look at your garden and do some tidying and grooming. Get rid of weeds as well as old pots or other garden debris that may be harboring slug populations. Try to dry out the area by thinning dense plantings and improving drainage. Reduce or eliminate mulch.

Failing to spot pests or diseases

When you see the plant in the nursery, it has lots of leaves and flower buds. But then you get it home and plant it in your windowbox, only to discover that the underside of almost every leaf is thick with aphids. Or you happen to notice with horror that the grape ivy plant you received as a gift is teeming with mealybugs. Untreated, an afflicted plant suffers and often dies. On its way out, it may spread its problem to any and all nearby plants.

THE RIGHT WAY TO DO IT In the shop—or, failing that, at home—inspect plants by turning over their leaves, looking closely at new growth, and peering into intersections of leaves and stems, all favorite places for insect pests to congregate. Sticky leaves or stippled ones covered with fine, whitish webs are also telltale signs. Also look for strangely discolored or misshapen leaves, which can be a sign of disease. (A few yellow leaves generally aren't a cause for worry.)

Make it a habit to quarantine newcomers for a few days or weeks. Spray them off outdoors or swish each one in a sink or bucketful of lukewarm water (hold soil in place with your fingers or a piece of paper 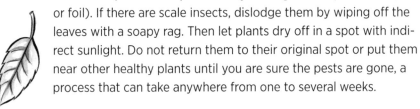 or foil). If there are scale insects, dislodge them by wiping off the leaves with a soapy rag. Then let plants dry off in a spot with indirect sunlight. Do not return them to their original spot or put them near other healthy plants until you are sure the pests are gone, a process that can take anywhere from one to several weeks.

IF I GOOFED, CAN I FIX IT? Start by bathing an afflicted plant. You may then spray with an insecticidal soap according to the label directions (these products contain fatty acids that eliminate lingering pests, are safe to use on any plant, and have low toxicity for people and pets). Or you can spot-treat delicate plants with Q-tips dipped in rubbing alcohol, which kills pests by dehydrating them.

Not identifying the culprit

Sometimes unwanted pests invade your garden or attack specific plants. By the time you notice, things don't look good. Leaves, buds, or flowers are chewed up, browned, or infested. A plant or patch may be on its last legs.

If you chop back or rip out an infected plant or area, you may not contain the problem. It can come back or continue damaging more plants if you don't treat it properly or thoroughly enough, or if you don't correctly dispose of affected plants or plant parts. If you spray willy-nilly, or with an inappropriate product, you may damage adjacent plants, kill beneficial insects, introduce toxins into your soil and water table, or create a hazard for yourself, your children, or your pets.

THE RIGHT WAY TO DO IT Know your enemy, and monitor your plants frequently so you can catch and act on potential problems. Learn what is and is not a pest; many insects in your yard neither help nor harm plants, while others are parasites or helpful predators. Look in reference books, view photos online, or show a sample critter or telltale damaged plant part to a more experienced gardener, nursery staff member, or landscape professional.

Carefully consider your control options. Small populations of some pests can be handpicked or knocked off with spray from the hose. Other effective tactics include using barriers like row covers or netting, traps or Tanglefoot which has an adhesive coating, or biological controls, or encouraging predators of the pest. Spray as a last resort, and follow label directions about dosage and timing to the letter.

IF I GOOFED, CAN I FIX IT? If, in your homicidal zeal to eradicate a garden pest, you fear you have damaged the environment or desirable plants, stop. Clean up with care. Read the product's label warnings if you haven't already, and if there isn't sufficient remedial information, go back to where you bought the product or research it online. Resolve, going forward, to be much more prudent with diagnosis and treatment.

Allowing tunneling rodents to invade

Moles, gophers, shrews, mice, voles—these creatures spend at least some of their time underground in tunnels. When they turn up in your garden, their activities can wreak havoc. Some may eat soil bugs but might also dine on beneficial earthworms. Some will heave up seedlings and sever tender roots as a result of their tunneling. A disfigured lawn is a sure giveaway that you have let the digging rodents get out of hand.

If you do not fight back, you will lose plants. Over time, your yard may become unattractive and unsafe for walking as it becomes pitted with holes, tunnels, and mounds.

THE RIGHT WAY TO DO IT Find out from your neighbors what sorts of critters have plagued their yards and lawns and keep a lookout. Take preventive steps. Build borders or trenches of stones, clay, or compacted soil around the areas you wish to protect. Or try burying small-mesh fencing that also stands a couple of inches above the soil surface. Either way, barriers need to go down about 2 feet to be truly effective.

IF I GOOFED, CAN I FIX IT? There are options if an invasion is underway. Try flushing the pests out of their tunnels with hose water, best done in the spring when their young are still in the nests. Try blocking exits by filling or stamping down holes (although there's no guarantee you'll get them all, or that you'll get the right ones). Some gardeners have tried smoke bombs, castor-oil solutions, and even chewing-gum traps, with mixed results. It helps to find out if your rodent is a meat eater or a vegetarian (carnivorous moles don't eat poisoned peanuts, for example). If you resort to trapping, place traps in main runs, which tend to be deeper under the ground, not in shallow, surface-feeding runs. Severe infestations in your yard and lawn call for stern and savvy action. Contact your nearest animal control officer for advice and help.

114

Trying to combat an infestation yourself

Because you're a do-it-yourselfer, or in the interest of saving money, you may try to treat an insect infestation on your own. In the case of Japanese beetles on your rosebushes or cutworms in the vegetable garden, there are certainly steps you can take. If you have serious infestations in bigger and more valuable plants, such as peach tree borers in your ornamental cherry tree or spider mites in your blue spruces, call in an expert—or risk losing the plant or watching the problem spread. Correct diagnosis is only part of the expert solution; proper treatment, applied safely and at the right time, can be beyond the ability of most of us.

THE RIGHT WAY TO DO IT Keep an eye on the health of all of your plants, large and small. If you observe symptoms that worry you (yellowing or prematurely dying foliage or needles, dying-back branches, suspected pests), don't wait long before acting. One season of trouble may be more than some plants can tolerate before failing.

Remember that a variety of stress factors cause decline. Plants that aren't getting the sun or the space they need, are suffering root damage, or would benefit from fertilizing and supplemental watering should get what they need so they are strong enough to resist pest (and disease) problems.

When you recognize a problem, call in an expert, such as a local landscaper or a professional arborist. Don't expect a diagnosis over the phone—she will need to see it. Ask what is required to treat it, then get an estimate for that work or determine whether it's something you can do.

IF I GOOFED, CAN I FIX IT? If, despite your best efforts, a plant continues to decline, you have two choices. You can belatedly call in expert help and heed his diagnosis and recommendations, or you can remove the plant. If you'd like to replace it, consider whether there might be a more suitable, hopefully less vulnerable, plant for the vacated spot.

PRUNING

GET A HANDLE ON CUTTING TOOLS AND PROPER TECHNIQUES.

Using the wrong tool

"That limb has to go—now," you mutter as you march in from the yard, grab the pruners, and go back out to take care of the matter. The branch is a little too thick for the tool and you end up making the cut by wiggling the pruners, changing positions, forcing and shimmying along the cut line, and tearing the bark. The inevitable result is a rough, ragged cut and a sloppy-looking stub. Not to mention your hand or wrist probably hurts (blisters, too?) and the tool may be loosened, dulled, or damaged.

Using a saw for a smaller job, or a dull saw, can have similarly bad consequences for you and the plant. Plus, it can slip and nick adjacent stems.

THE RIGHT WAY TO DO IT Generally speaking, use smaller tools for smaller jobs and bigger tools for bigger jobs. Hand shears and pruners are best for taking off branches and stems up to ½ inch in diameter. For jobs involving growth larger than this, up to about 1½ inches in diameter, use loppers—the longer handles and heavier blades have more cutting power. If you need to take out high limbs, use a ladder or invest in a pole pruner.

Bigger branches require a saw. Always use a pruning saw, not one meant for carpentry projects. The teeth on pruning saws are designed to work on green (wet, live) wood without clogging or gumming up; woodworking saws are effective only on dry wood. A chainsaw is meant for the biggest jobs. Remember to keep your pruning tools sharp and clean so they cut effectively and do not spread disease from one plant to another.

IF I GOOFED, CAN I FIX IT? If you realize you are using the wrong tool while in the middle of a pruning project, stop and get the right one. As for repair work on poorly executed cuts, don't make it worse. Using the correct tool, cut back past the damage as well as you can.

Pruning at the wrong time of year

If you cut back a tree, shrub, or rosebush in the fall (when it may be easier to see and critique a plant's outline, or you may not be as busy), your cuts expose plant tissues that can be damaged, frozen, or blackened by cold. The cuts might also cause a plant to send out a flush of new tender growth that cannot tolerate colder air and will suffer frost damage or get killed. Pruning back flowering shrubs and

 trees must be properly timed so you don't inadvertently remove the buds set for next year's show. Hacking back an unruly forsythia or lilac in late summer or fall, for example, reduces the bulk but also destroys all chances of the traditional shower of blooms next spring.

THE RIGHT WAY TO DO IT There are some general rules about proper timing; bear in mind that certain types of plants (hydrangeas, clematis) may have different requirements within their own species, and it is best to double-check in a reference book or with a landscape professional.

Late winter, when the weather has warmed up slightly but there are no signs of new growth or swelling buds, is a good time to prune and shape roses, broadleaf evergreens, vines, and some flowering trees. Springtime pruning should be less dramatic, more along the lines of shaping and removing winter-damaged branches. In early summer, when growth is in full swing, you can shear evergreens and hedges, as well as shrubs that have just finished flowering (catch them before they start making buds for next year's show). Trees that bleed sap (birches and maples) are best pruned in late summer. Fall pruning, as mentioned, can be risky, although some shrubs and woody vines will tolerate moderate cutting before the weather gets too cold.

IF I GOOFED, CAN I FIX IT? Healthy plants, luckily, are fairly forgiving. If you overpruned, or took off most or all of the flower buds, the plant is not ruined forever; it's just compromised for a year. Take good care of it and it should recover. In the meantime, find out the best time to prune it, and mend your ways accordingly.

BRANCH COLLAR

UNDERCUT

UNDERCUT 12–24 IN. UP
FROM THE BRANCH COLLAR.

SECOND CUT

MAKE SECOND CUT FROM
THE TOP ALL THE WAY
THROUGH THE BRANCH, 2–3
IN. ABOVE FIRST CUT.

FINAL CUT

MAKE FINAL CUT JUST
BEYOND BRANCH COLLAR.
SUPPORT STUB SO IT DOES
NOT TEAR BARK.

THE RIGHT WAY TO REMOVE A BRANCH

Failing to leave a collar when removing a branch

The wrong way to cut a branch is straight through the limb, which causes splitting or tearing, often all the way back to the bigger branch or trunk it is attached to. Proper removal of the remaining stub is important. Scalping it off flat against the originating branch or trunk, or taking off the collar, is detrimental to the tree's health because the collar contains trunk or parent branch tissue. It also forms a natural protection zone that prevents infection from spreading back into the trunk. Taking off the collar can also cause sprouts (suckers) to grow in the vicinity of the wound. If the cut was intended to thin, you certainly don't want the tree to generate a flurry of new growth.

THE RIGHT WAY TO DO IT Always remove a tree limb in stages with two cuts. Pick a point several inches to a foot out, and make an undercut about a quarter of the way through the branch. Then saw through from the top, 1 inch or more further out. This safely severs or snaps off the limb. Remove the remaining stub just beyond the ridge of the collar.

You do not need to dress the wound with tar, clay, manure, or paint. Modern research has shown that a good pruning cut allows the tree to seal off the wound on its own and prevent the spread of infection. A dressing can even be harmful by keeping the wound moist, which disease-causing microorganisms relish.

IF I GOOFED, CAN I FIX IT? A left-behind stub tends to die back. At best, this delays healing over of the wound; at worst, it sends decay back into the main tree. Cut back to the collar, but don't try to gouge out the dead portion inside. Eventually the tree should heal over and envelop the wound. If you or a pruner who preceded you took off the collar, this is unfortunate but need not be fatal. Keep an eye on the spot and clip off any sprouts that appear. If disease or insects appear to move in, call an arborist for advice.

Making a bad cut

In the world of shrub pruning, a bad cut is one that won't heal or doesn't heal well. Your intervention—removing a diseased or damaged branch, letting more air and light into a plant, shaping—can end up doing more harm than good.

If you leave a stub, new bark cannot grow over the wound and rot will eventually work its way into healthy plant tissue. This is also true for slender branches when you cut too far from the nearest bud; the dead stub tends to rot back. In both cases, while it lasts, the overlong stub looks unattractive on the plant. When you chop off a branch or

122

stem too close to a bud, however, the bud won't receive enough sap and will dry out or risk damage from freezing temperatures. A flat-topped cut is detrimental because it is slow to dry out after a rain, and rot and disease can move in. Plus, it looks stubby and ugly.

THE RIGHT WAY TO DO IT When cutting back stems and small branches on a shrub, the best cut is an angled or slanted one made above the nearest healthy or promising bud. The slant looks better and dries out faster after a rain. Positioning your cut about ¼ inch above the bud inspires new growth.

If removing a tree limb, cut back to a live branch or the main trunk. If the branch is heavy, make the cut in stages so it won't break and split back into the next branch or the trunk; cut from below first, then finish the job by sawing from above and 1 inch or more beyond the lower cut. One final note: Always use a sharp cutting tool, whether a pruner, lopper, or saw. Dull blades work poorly and slowly, mashing plant tissues. A clean, sharp cut is a good cut.

IF I GOOFED, CAN I FIX IT? Recut, if you can, following these instructions. The plant may not look as good or as balanced as you had initially hoped, but it should recover in time. If you fear you have really damaged a plant or tree, get professional advice or help.

Not knowing when to call an arborist

Hubris is never a good quality in a gardener, and it's dangerous to take on a big job like reducing the bulk of a large tree or removing a heavy branch that's overhanging wires or the garage. You can fall, wrench muscles, harm the tree, accidentally drop a branch on a roof or car, cut yourself, and so on.

If you know what you're doing, you may be able to prune a fruit tree so it will bear good crops, fashion an espalier or topiary, or rejuvenate a badly overgrown or diseased tree. Tackling these jobs without knowledge or seasoned advice can lead to a botched job, perhaps past the point of saving the plant or attaining the result you want.

THE RIGHT WAY TO DO IT Lacking the nerve, strength, or proper tools to undertake a big pruning job is one thing; lacking the knowledge of how to do it safely and effectively is worse. When in doubt, or if you're out of your league, call in a professional arborist. If you are trying to save money, consult for advice only, but be prepared to hire him if he recommends that you don't do the job.

To find a good professional to prune for you, search your Yellow Pages or online, ask friends and neighbors, or inquire at your local nursery. Before the visit, ask if he is insured and which professional memberships he belongs to. You are looking for International Society of Arboriculture (ISA), the Tree Care Industry Association (TCIA), or the American Society of Consulting Arborists (ASCA). Two final, useful insider tips: Avoid arborists who advertise topping, a practice that has been discredited, and don't hire those who climb trees by using spikes, which are harmful to trees. As when hiring any contractor, discuss the project thoroughly, ask for and check references, and get your agreement (and payment estimates and arrangements) in writing.

IF I GOOFED, CAN I FIX IT? Experienced professional arborists know how to judge, and repair, botched pruning jobs—call, eat humble pie, and try to save your tree.

ROSES
SPUR A GLORIOUS SHOW FROM THESE SOMETIMES DAUNTING BEAUTIES.

Desperate spraying

Roses, particularly the older yet still popular hybrid teas, do get pests and diseases. When you find your bush infested with aphids or Japanese beetles, or mildewed, or marred by blackspot, it's only natural to be upset. You may storm down to the garden center, scoop up a can of a product whose label mentions treating rose problems, and blanket the bush with spray. But unless you have the right product, it won't help—and could even be harmful. Even if you choose a spray that is clearly labeled for the culprit or disease, if you don't follow the label directions regarding timing and amount (not to mention safe application), it won't be as effective as you want it to be.

THE RIGHT WAY TO DO IT Take a more methodical approach. First, examine the plant carefully, including under the leaves, to accurately diagnose the problem and assess its scope. Next, pick off all afflicted plant parts, as well as any on the ground at its base, and throw them in the trash.

Then research remedies. Japanese beetles can be handpicked and drowned in a bucket of soapy water (do this in the evening, when they congregate). You can blast off aphids with a spray from the hose. Common rose diseases respond to correctly applied sprays, but also to careful sanitation and proper care (including watering on the ground so the leaves don't get splashed). If you decide to spray, try less-toxic treatments first and always read and heed the label. If the material is at all dangerous—this sort of caution will be noted on the label—protect yourself with eyewear, gloves, long pants, and long sleeves.

IF I GOOFED, CAN I FIX IT? With renewed attention and prudent care, a rose will often recover from a common pest or malady; if it doesn't, it's time to replace it, possibly with a tougher, more resistant variety. Let this be a reminder to take good care of your rose plants so they are less vulnerable to problems. Desperate spraying is not only foolish and wasteful, it doesn't remedy the actual problem.

Choosing a disease-prone variety

Let's be honest: we love, and grow, roses primarily for their gorgeous flowers. It's all too easy to choose one based on the beauty of its blossoms. Once in the ground and growing for a while, the plant indeed produces the blooms you were dreaming of. But soon you begin to see its flaws, mostly in the growth or the leaves, but possibly in buds and blooms, too. Your plant has blackspot (worst in hot, humid

 weather) or suffers from mildew (which thrives in dry conditions). Or it may even have an incurable rose virus, such as Rose Mosaic Virus (RMV; deformed new growth, yellow mottling on leaves) or Rose Rosette Disease (RRD; distorted, crinkled leaves, dark reddish-purple color all year, rapid aberrant growth and elongation). If caught early, you may be able to fight the common diseases. There is no remedy for the viruses except ripping out and disposing of the afflicted plants.

THE RIGHT WAY TO DO IT Check with a local rose expert before you buy or plant a rose, and tell her you want one resistant to rose diseases prevalent in your area. Or get assistance at your nursery from someone who knows roses (reputable nurseries will sell only virus-free stock). For all the susceptible roses, there are plenty of worthy and gorgeous tough ones whose foliage creates a handsome foil for those beautiful blooms.

IF I GOOFED, CAN I FIX IT? Legions of rose lovers have put up with common rose diseases by picking off and getting rid of affected leaves and plant parts or spraying—they love the flowers too much to forgo them. If you are among the smitten, undertake prevention and control wisely. Diagnose the disease correctly, then research the remedies, which can vary from spraying with baking-soda solution to using a fungicide or other chemical control. Get good advice on what to do, and when, from your local consulting rosarian (see the American Rose Society's website) or rose club.

Remember, too, that practicing good sanitation (get rid of afflicted plant parts), judicious pruning (to improve air circulation in and near the plant), and watering on the ground (rather than splashing the leaves) can help.

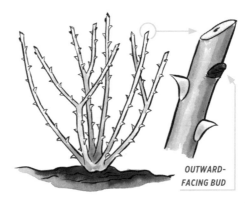

OUTWARD-
FACING BUD

THE RIGHT WAY TO TRIM A ROSE

Pruning your rose the wrong way

When a rose outgrows its space, sending its thorny canes taller or wider than you want them to go, you'll want to prune. Or perhaps you wish to shape an unruly rose to achieve a tidy, formal look. Either way, it's important to prune at the right time and in the right way. While it's often tempting to clip and shape a rosebush in the fall as the leaves drop and the profile of the plant is more obvious, this is the worst time in colder climates. Cold and freezing air can damage the fresh cuts (causing blackening and dieback) and stunt or kill the fresh flush of new growth that cutting often inspires.

Improperly executed cuts can also mar the look of a rose plant. Cuts made too close to a bud cause it to shrivel up and die. Cuts made over an inward-facing bud encourage growth in the wrong direction, contributing to a crowded, tangled bush. Overzealously cutting long-stemmed bouquets of blooming roses in the summer can scalp a plant.

THE RIGHT WAY TO DO IT Generally speaking, the best time to prune most roses is in early spring, just as the buds are beginning to swell and after all chance of hard frost is past. (In warmer climates, where freezing is not an issue, you may safely prune in fall or winter.) Start by taking out winter-damaged and very old canes at the ground. If the plant is grafted, closely cut off unwelcome suckers emanating from below the graft. Next, remove branches that are rubbing, crossed, or too close together. Shorten trailing stems. Aim for a half-dozen or so healthy canes, shortening them to about a foot high. As spring arrives, the revitalized plant will surge into fresh new growth.

A proper cut is made with a sharp, clean pair of pruners or loppers, on a slant, about ¼ inch above an outward-facing bud. If a branch has leafed out, cut just above a five-leaflet side stem.

IF I GOOFED, CAN I FIX IT? Give an improperly pruned rose a year off, during which time it will hopefully generate some new growth and recover, even if it doesn't look great. Then prune early the following spring as described.

Planting your rose the wrong way

A rose planted in poor-quality or poorly drained soil, or in a spot with not enough sunshine, sulks. It may not die, but it will never produce lush, healthy foliage or lots of pretty blossoms, and its growth may be stunted or look lanky. A rose planted too deeply struggles because its root system is not getting sufficient water and oxygen, and it can suffocate. One planted too shallowly, however, has a root system that is too exposed.

The situation is further complicated if you are planting a grafted rose. Set the plant in too shallowly, and it may produce unwanted canes off the rootstock rather than the desirable grafted plant.

THE RIGHT WAY TO DO IT Whether you are planting a bareroot rose or a potted one, set it in the ground at the same depth at which it was growing—there will be a line evident on the main stem. Fine-tune this directive if it is a grafted plant. In mild areas, position the graft union slightly above the soil surface; in colder climates, bury it slightly below the soil surface.

Plant a rose in a sunny, prepared site in good, organically rich soil that drains well. For a bareroot one, create a cone of soil in the hole and gently array the roots over it. For a potted rose, take time to gently tease the roots loose so they can grow into the surrounding soil. To avoid air pockets, backfill the hole about halfway, then water well and let it soak in before continuing. Make adjustments as needed at the end of the job, adding or removing soil until the plant is at the desired depth.

IF I GOOFED, CAN I FIX IT? Assuming the rose is not on its last legs after you realize you planted it incorrectly, dig it out. Temporarily move the plant into a large pot or protect the root system from drying out by laying a damp cloth over it while you prepare a new hole, in a better spot if necessary. Replant as described.

Letting a rose produce suckers

Something is obviously wrong when, one or two seasons into life in your yard, a rose you chose for its beauty starts putting out wayward stems with thin, small, or unattractive leaves, shooting up suckers from the base, and producing flowers that are not what you expected. You're so disappointed and disgusted, you're ready to tear it out.

Were you sold a mislabeled plant? Maybe. But more likely you didn't protect the graft, and winter's cold, or something else—a wayward string trimmer?—knocked off or killed the grafted or top plant. What you are seeing is growth produced by the rootstock. Rose rootstocks are not chosen for their beauty, but for the cold-hardiness, uniformity, and even disease-resistance they can confer to the more attractive plant grafted on top.

THE RIGHT WAY TO DO IT Gardeners who grow roses in colder climates have two choices. If you want to enjoy a rose that is grafted atop a rootstock (if you are not sure if the one you are contemplating is grafted, ask or look for the telltale bulge in the stem just above the roots), plant it correctly. Set it so the graft, or bulge, is slightly below the soil level, and mulch several inches deep over the plant to help it through the winter months.

Alternatively, shop for an own-root rose. Many shrub roses are in this category, including lovely heirloom varieties. Make sure it is rated hardy in your climate zone. If winter kills or harms the top, when the roots send up new growth, it will be the same plant you expected and wanted.

IF I GOOFED, CAN I FIX IT? If you planted a grafted rose too shallowly and winter (or a mishap) killed the top, there is no recourse. Tear out the remains, including all of the unwanted rootstock, and start over. Invest in a cold-hardy own-root rose, or plant a grafted rose properly and be sure to mulch it well come winter.

SHRUBS

MINIMIZE MAINTENANCE AND MAXIMIZE THE LOOK YOU WANT.

The foundation-shrubs blues

Whether you inherited or planted a line of foundation shrubs, you may feel ambivalent about them. On the one hand, they probably do their job of covering over or distracting from the unattractive foundation of your home or garage, perhaps while also providing some welcome privacy. On the other hand, they may need more maintenance than you bargained for, or might be growing too bushy or too tall and crowding the front of your home or blocking windows and light.

THE RIGHT WAY TO DO IT Installing foundation plants can be a major investment in time, money, and effort. Examine the site before you break ground or buy any plants. Planting close to a structure can be tricky. Does the soil and drainage situation need improvement? Do your roof or gutters dump rainwater on the site or ferry the water away (which means you will have to water the plants)? Adjacent walls, depending on what they are made of, whether they are painted, and how close the shrubs ultimately crowd them, can get damp and moldy or begin to harbor wood-nibbling insects. Be sure to allow sufficient room for air circulation and access for any repairs to the house or cellar.

Don't be seduced into buying lots of inexpensive plants for this job. Choose ones that are handsome and grow densely and slowly (so you don't have to prune often), and are naturally shorter or dwarf varieties. Over time, taller shrubs outgrow their space.

If someone else already installed unsuitable foundation plants, you're faced with either hacking them back to a better size or removing and possibly replacing them. To help you decide, find out what they are, how big they ultimately grow, and how likely they are to respond to drastic pruning.

IF I GOOFED, CAN I FIX IT? If removing an entire line of too-big or ugly foundation plants is daunting, you might try thinning—good pruning of individual plants, or even removing every other one. Plants that are too bulky can sometimes be brought down to size, although this is not a lasting solution.

Choosing the wrong plants for a hedge

A bad hedge plant is one that doesn't do the intended job. It grows too slowly when you wanted a fast screen. It never gets tall enough, or it remains too short. It needs constant clipping to keep from looking ratty. It doesn't grow densely enough and people can see through it.

THE RIGHT WAY TO DO IT Shop purposefully. Pick out plants for a hedge based on what you expect or need, not because they look attractive or are inexpensive or on sale. A good, logical method is to consider the natural conditions (shade? sun? soil type and quality?), measure the intended spot, and research some good candidates (not just in books, catalogs, or online, but alive and growing in your neighborhood or area parks).

Visit the nursery last. If your goal is quick cover, choose a fast-grower (such as privet, myrtle, or cherry laurel) or spend the money on more mature plants. Before purchasing and planting a new hedge, it's wise to get advice from the nursery or a reputable landscaper regarding how many plants you'll need and how closely to plant them in order to achieve the intended look. Don't neglect soil improvement or any needed drainage alterations, either, which is so much easier to do before installing the plants.

IF I GOOFED, CAN I FIX IT? A too-thin or scraggly hedge can sometimes be remedied by wedging in additional, matching plants or by stepping up water, fertilizer, and shearing efforts to encourage denser growth. Extra-diligent care can also spur a slow grower along. The worst-case scenario is to rip out the entire hedge and start over.

Overzealous cutting back

Those big rhododendrons off the front porch have grown too tall and broad, blocking light and obscuring the view. Plus, they have bare knees and are no longer doing their job of covering the foundation. Or the hedge along the side or front of the yard, left unchecked, has gotten entirely too high. The yard feels hemmed in, too dark, and claustrophobic.

You'd like to keep the plants, but shorten them. Simply chopping them back—say, by half—is usually a recipe for disaster. If the plants don't die from major surgery, they tend not to revive well (new growth is reluctant to appear or is thin). And it looks like a hack job.

THE RIGHT WAY TO DO IT In the case of an overlarge, unkempt rhododendron, play it safe and take out only a few older branches each year over a period of several years. Meanwhile, encourage denser growth by pinching off new shoots in the spring before the leaves fully unfurl. While you're at it, nip or pinch off terminal growth buds to inspire more branching.

Generally speaking, you are better off cutting back most other shrubs within a foot of the ground. A year or two before you do this, start taking especially good care of the plants—watering, fertilizing, and mulching them well—so they are as healthy and hearty as possible. Do the cutback in late winter or early spring, then lavish more good care so the plants rejuvenate. When new growth appears, be diligent about pruning and pinching to encourage and maintain this new, improved smaller size. Most deciduous and broad-leaf evergreen shrubs respond well, given time, to such dramatic pruning (needled evergreens, junipers, and boxwood do not).

IF I GOOFED, CAN I FIX IT? For most shrubs, yes. Follow the directions about drastic early-season pruning. Try it with a hacked rhododendron, too, as you have nothing to lose. If the project is daunting or dispiriting, you can always dig out the gangly shrubs and invest in new, smaller-profile plants.

Turning a shrub into bad topiary

It has long been the fashion in some places to clip shrubs into neat, mannered, or eccentric shapes. A casual or uneducated attempt at shaping tends to lead to an odd-looking plant or a misshapen specimen.

If you start shaping when a plant is older, the project is more difficult because branches are thicker and a growth pattern is established. Well-intentioned shaping cuts can end up looking like a bad haircut from which the plant is slow to recover. If you are impatient and try to create a shape quickly—that is, in one growing season—you are also often doomed to disappointment because the most attractive, densest-growing shapes take several years to come to fruition. Finally, not every plant type is amenable to shaping, and no matter what you do or how carefully you do it, the result will be unsatisfactory (pines, spruces, and firs, for example, aren't very cooperative).

THE RIGHT WAY TO DO IT For homeowners with limited time and patience, a shrub pruned to look handsome but not overly formal will look compatible with the rest of the yard. Your pruning should enhance the shrub's appearance and health. Capitalize on its best feature. For example, prune your lilac to control its height, so the gorgeous blossoms are at eye (and nose) level rather than out of reach. Prune a hemlock sparingly to inspire denser growth, so its naturally soft, graceful profile reaches its full potential.

If your goal is a true piece of garden topiary (on the order of the great estates of England or the Maryland hunt country), research the techniques and possibilities. Then choose an appropriate plant, and start young, when its growth is most amenable to sculpting and better able to recover from cuts. Suitable evergreens include hemlock, holly, yew, boxwood, and cypress. Deciduous plants that also make nice topiary candidates are cotoneaster, privet, Japanese maples, and pyracantha. Give such a project plenty of time—years, in fact.

IF I GOOFED, CAN I FIX IT? A misshapen plant or one with gaps is not impossible to repair and reshape, but you will have to be patient. If you are unhappy with your work, leave the plant alone for a season or two. Give it plenty of water and perhaps some fertilizer so it grows healthy and lush and its natural growth habit is able to reassert itself. Only then should you resume attempts to shape it, this time in accordance with what is best for it and for your garden's appearance.

Pruning the flower buds off a shrub

This is a common gardening mistake, but that may be little solace when you discover your error. No matter how adeptly or clumsily you pruned a shrub in your yard, if you did so at the wrong time—when new flower buds were forming, or had already formed, for next year's show—you cut them off. When blooming time comes around again, the show is greatly diminished or even nonexistent. Really disappointing.

THE RIGHT WAY TO DO IT The first lesson is that most flowering shrubs don't need much pruning. Those that get lanky or bulky, such as lilacs, viburnums, and honeysuckles, should be reined in from time to time. But most will get by with occasional (once every few years) thinning to remove wood that is growing too thickly or to take out older branches that have clearly lost their vitality.

The second lesson is trickier. If you decide to do some cutting, you need to determine the correct timing. Does your shrub bloom on new wood produced the same year (elder, beautyberry, crape myrtle, PeeGee hydrangea, rose-of-Sharon, spirea, and viburnum)? Prune when the plant is dormant in late fall or late winter, and it will still have plenty of opportunity to make a good show. Does your shrub bloom on old wood that grew during the previous season (forsythia, kerria, mock orange, smokebush, and lilac)? Promptly prune right after the blooms fade. New buds and branches for next year's display can form after your cutting is done.

IF I GOOFED, CAN I FIX IT? What's done is done, but unless your pruning was drastic or extensive, the shrub should recover in a season or two. Show your remorse and help the shrub along by taking good care of it: provide supplemental water and fertilizer as needed, and carefully take out broken, diseased, or dead branches.

SOIL

RESPECT AND WORK WITH YOUR GARDEN'S FOUNDATION, AND AVOID MANY HEARTACHES.

Trying to garden in compacted garden soil

You might have suspected something was amiss when you dug to install new plants, and the shovel or trowel had a hard time penetrating. Or you might suspect compacted soil if water runs right off or sinks in slowly, indicating there are few available air spaces, either because of parched ground or extremely saturated soil. Neither environment is good for most plants. Their roots will struggle for moisture, oxygen, and nutrients, and will show their distress aboveground by slumping, failing to produce new growth or flowers or fruit, browning and drying, and eventually keeling over.

THE RIGHT WAY TO DO IT Some parts of your yard are inevitably going to have compacted soil, unless you are willing and able to make necessary changes to improve or shield them. Trafficked areas, such as paths, always get beaten down as people and pets repeatedly walk over them, but frequent passages by a garden cart, a wheelbarrow, bicycles, and small tractors will also contribute to the problem. A location where heavy objects, such as cars and trash bins, are kept is bound to have dense, compacted, unfriendly soil.

The answer is easy: designate some areas for traffic, and others for plants. And the obvious corollary? Don't plant in compacted soil. If you'd like to plant an area later but need to use it or walk over it for a while, lay down and travel over boards, which will redistribute your weight more evenly and tend to mitigate soil compaction.

IF I GOOFED, CAN I FIX IT? Plant rescue may be possible. Remove the struggling plants, replant them in a more hospitable location, and hope they recover and begin to thrive in their new home.

Alternatively, remove the beleaguered plants temporarily, loosen the soil and mix in some good decomposed organic matter to improve soil structure and fertility, and return them to these improved growing conditions. Rope, fence off, or define the area with edging, route traffic around or away from the area, or otherwise prevent future compaction.

Not preparing the soil before planting

You've done everything else right—chosen a decent-quality plant, provided it with a sunny or shady spot as needed, planted it with care, watered and tended it. And yet, in a few days or weeks, the plant looks terrible or simply quits and dies.

There is no guarantee that native soil is any good. It could be compacted or gritty. It might be contaminated with road salt, motor oil, or other environmental pollutants. It may simply be depleted or infertile. No matter the reason, a new plant cannot successfully send its roots into lousy soil and get the nourishment it needs to grow and prosper.

THE RIGHT WAY TO DO IT Make it your standard practice to improve soil before adding any plant at any time. Most popular garden plants like well-drained, moderately organic soil, which has a rich, crumbly texture and is dark in color. To get it from any other state to something resembling this ideal, add organic matter such as compost, bagged dehydrated cow manure, or chopped-up fall leaves.

Dig down to a depth of 6 to 8 inches, the extent of most plants' root systems. Go deeper if installing a bigger plant. Mix in the organic matter well—like cake batter, you'll have to determine the best recipe. Add more in very bad soil, less in soil that appears halfway decent. If the native soil seems truly awful, dig it out by making a hole or trench, and replace it altogether.

Only now should you add a new plant and follow through with good care. Continue adding organic matter in the fall and again the following spring. Soil and plants consume organic matter, so this becomes an ongoing, nurturing practice.

IF I GOOFED, CAN I FIX IT? If a plant put into bad soil is still alive, dig it out and set it aside, either in a pot of soil mix or with a damp cloth over its roots to keep them from dehydrating. Then improve its hole or bed with organic matter as described, replant it, water and care for it, and hope you intervened in time.

WHAT ELSE?

Sometimes amending is not necessary and can even cause harm. A tree or native plant tends to do best in native ground. A single new perennial, or two, may do just fine with a little compost added to the planting hole rather than a wholesale upgrade of the entire bed. (Vegetable gardens, however, almost always need improved soil.)

Not knowing what your soil is like

Some plants prefer certain soils. If you plant lavender in moist, rich, acidic soil, it will flower poorly, produce weak foliage, and generally sulk, for it wants well-drained, slightly alkaline ground. Conversely, if you give a camellia a sandy, dry site, the shallow roots cannot access the water and nutrients they need to supply to the plant. The leaves and the flower petals will dry out, and the plant will decline and die.

THE RIGHT WAY TO DO IT Never add a plant to your yard without knowing if you have the right soil type to support it. Yes, you can supply special soil for a special plant, but it is so much easier to make a good match at the beginning.

If you don't know what kind of soil you have (rich or lean, moist or dry, alkaline or acidic), it's not hard to find out: conduct a soil test. You can get a formal kit at a garden center or via the Cooperative Extension Service; these kits come with complete instructions and involve digging up soil samples from various parts of your yard and sending them to a lab for analysis. Or you can do less precise identification. The plants prospering there now, including weeds and ones you have not planted, can provide clues. Look up what they prefer. Alternatively, ask a professional landscaper to recommend soil improvements as well as plants that ought to do well in your yard. If you don't want to fuss, your best bet is native plants, which are already adapted to local soils and climate. Ask for them at your local garden center.

IF I GOOFED, CAN I FIX IT? If a plant is unhappy, take it out and grow it in a pot of appropriate soil, give it away, or toss it on the compost pile. Then plant something that likes the soil you already have.

Digging or tilling too much

Turning over the soil every spring is a popular garden ritual, so entrenched that few gardeners ever question it. There is something satisfying about breaking ground and feeling your shovel slice into the earth. But it's also hard work, especially tough on your back, and it can be distressing to watch what often follows—a weed explosion. Weed seeds that had been dozing underground are now exposed to air and light, and once stirred, they wake up and grow.

Ritual spring digging also delays planting, because you cannot dig until the soil dries out a bit or it will be compacted, not to mention a messy job. Furthermore, soil bacteria and fungi burst into activity after tilling, consuming organic matter. You want them to settle down, which can take a few weeks, before adding any seeds or plants to the area.

THE RIGHT WAY TO DO IT Delay digging until later in the spring, when the soil is not mucky. The object of digging should be to get rid of existing vegetation or to turn under a deliberately planted cover crop. Another benefit is aerating compacted soil so new seeds and roots

146

can become established. Mulch the area immediately after digging to discourage weeds and conserve soil moisture, and replenish as needed when you finally plant.

Some gardeners believe in skipping digging altogether and following nature's way of letting humus settle on and into the ground over time. They note that digging disrupts natural soil layers and drainage capability, as overdug soil drains too quickly. If your garden soil is in good shape to begin with, try taking a year off from ritual spring digging, but don't forget to mulch.

IF I GOOFED, CAN I FIX IT? Let the ground rest and recover. Don't plant anything right away, but mulch with organic matter, such as compost or chopped-up leaves, to smother weeds. Later in the season, gently scoot the mulch aside, add some organic matter to the soil, then try planting.

Gardening in contaminated or bad soil

Perhaps you inherited tainted soil from a previous occupant, or someone in your household has rendered an area toxic for plants. They will struggle and die, or you will be left wondering what is wrong or, if the crops are edible, whether they are safe to eat. Among the toxins that are cause for concern are: motor oil and other petroleum products; cleaning solutions, especially bleach; pesticides, including rat poison and flea killers; and lead, usually from paint that has flaked off an old building or fence.

Pressure-treated lumber, often used for garden structures and projects, contains chemicals (including arsenic and copper) that leach into garden soil over time. Don't grow vegetables or fruits close to this wood.

THE RIGHT WAY TO DO IT Never deliberately plant anything in a contaminated or suspect area. Don't eat food crops that appear to be growing in such a spot. To identify the scope and seriousness of the contamination, conduct a soil test. Your local Cooperative Extension Service will have kits and information, and can make recommendations or suggest remedies. If you or someone in your household needs to discard a toxic substance safely, your municipality's solid-waste program can advise you or even take it off your hands. Don't get in the habit of dumping in your own yard, behind the garage, or in an unused or overgrown area.

IF I GOOFED, CAN I FIX IT? If the dumping has already occurred, stop using the area as a place to grow anything unless or until it is cleaned up. Cover it over or block access to it. Cleanup can be as simple as diluting the area with hose water and as ambitious as digging up a wide area of bad soil and carting it to a disposal site. First identify the toxin, then get advice from your municipality's solid-waste program, as you may not be able to handle it on your own. In the meantime, perhaps you can pretty up the area by placing potted plants on-site or growing plants in raised beds bordered by stones or untreated lumber.

Struggling with waterlogged soil

Maybe it's obvious that a certain bed or corner of the yard is soggy because of standing water or moisture-loving weeds like watercress or sedges. You tear out these unwanted plants and try a few colorful flowers, but they don't prosper or they succumb to rot.

It's also common to find out the hard way that an area has sodden soil. You plant some bulbs, or even a tough perennial like Shasta daisy, and a wet, cold winter reveals that the area is low and water is draining into it and sitting there. The plants you introduced then fail because of the lousy drainage.

THE RIGHT WAY TO DO IT You have two choices. You can try to keep the moisture away, diverting incoming water or creating pebble-filled drainage basins or trenches in the vicinity. While you're at it, dig in some organic matter to lighten the soil's texture and provide a little oxygen and space for the root systems of plants you want to grow there.

If this seems like too much trouble, or if your remedial efforts don't succeed, your best bet is to plant the area with moisture-loving plants. Among annuals, this includes angelonia, impatiens, and even pansies.

Perennials that relish damp ground include bee balm, cardinal flower, and crocosmia. If the area is truly sodden for much of the growing

season, try various irises, mint, or the colorful, ground-covering chameleon plant (*Houttuynia cordata*). Do a little research or ask for more ideas at your favorite nursery—there are many fine choices. Just bear in mind that plants known to relish damp growing conditions can and will take over an area. At least they will be ones you want, though, and not unwelcome weeds.

IF I GOOFED, CAN I FIX IT? If you planted unsuitable plants in a damp area, don't fight a losing battle. Take them out while they are still alive and give them a more appropriate home elsewhere in your garden.

TOOLS

MAKING A MATCH BETWEEN TASK AND EQUIPMENT MAKES A HUGE DIFFERENCE.

Injuring trees with a string trimmer or weed whacker

Maybe it's because running around the edges of the lawn and beds with a string trimmer is the last thing you do after a long, tiring day of yardwork, but sloppy wielding of this tool is a common mishap. It's easy to let the heavy-duty nylon string nick or slice the trunks of trees it comes near. Enough, or repeated, damage, renders the bark—this season's growing layer—compromised or dead. You can maim or even kill a tree, especially a young, slender one, with a string trimmer.

THE RIGHT WAY TO DO IT Remove all grass in a protective ring around a tree trunk, then lay down bark chips or other weed- and grass-smothering mulch. A safe buffer zone for most trees is between 6 and 12 inches out from the trunk. Alternatively, for vulnerable trees in or next to the lawn, give the trunks a wide berth on the first pass with your lawn mower, then use the trimmer. Hold the cutting head parallel to the ground. If you work carefully, you should be able to keep that whipping line away from tree trunks. Obviously, this cautious approach will not cut back the tufts of grass right against the trunk. If this bothers you, cut back the growth with hand clippers.

All this being said, you should never use the trimmer around the base of young trees, whose cambium—its outer, growing layer—has a hard time recovering from chops and nicks.

IF I GOOFED, CAN I FIX IT? If your string trimmer has harmed the bark of a young tree, or even a more mature one, there is no quick cure. Stop the practice, and watch for a few months or a season to see if the tree heals over the wounds and recovers. If it does, install a mulch buffer zone as described.

Trying to remove a large limb with loppers

Even before you try to take off that wayward, dead, or storm-broken branch, you have an inkling this project might not go well. Wielding a pair of long-handled loppers, you slice into the wood, twisting it bit by bit as you work your way around the limb. You squeeze hard, grit your teeth, and curse, but you persist. It's more of an effort than you bargained for.

Finally, the branch yields to your clumsy surgery. It snaps and tears, ripping off bark as it falls to the ground and leaving a sloppy wound at the cutting site. You can't even finish off or neaten up the job with this tool. And your loppers are now loose and out of alignment, and won't be good for their intended use of slicing slim branches no more than 1½ inches in diameter. Oops.

THE RIGHT WAY TO DO IT Branches larger than 1½ inches in diameter cannot effectively be removed with loppers. Use a sharp-toothed pruning saw instead. For limbs up to about 3 inches in diameter, a simple Grecian saw is ideal, as it has a curved blade and teeth set to cut on the pull stroke. This common garden saw cuts quickly and well, can be deployed in tight places, and often comes with a handy safety and storage feature—the blade folds back into the handle (just be sure to wipe it clean of sap, sawdust, and dirt first). Alternatively, and for limbs larger than 3 inches, you can't go wrong with a bow saw. The blade will cut on both the push and pull strokes.

IF I GOOFED, CAN I FIX IT? Deploy a pruning saw to neaten the sloppy cut as best you can. If you cannot mend your damaged loppers by tightening the bolt where the blades meet, take them to a repair shop to see if they can be fixed. Either you or the shop should also clean the cutting surfaces and perhaps even sharpen them so the abused tool can live to be of service another day.

Using a spade or shovel as a crowbar

Among the heaviest projects a gardener can undertake are clearing out a new area in order to install a new bed or plants, and ejecting obstructions such as large rocks, stumps, and unwanted roots. Sometimes these jobs go together and sometimes not, but either way it's hard work. Your back aches, your hands blister, and the sweat pours down. Using the wrong tool makes the work that much harder. For example, wedging a spade or shovel under a stubborn boulder and trying to lever it out may result in a bowed or snapped handle, or the

blade detaching, or both. Meanwhile, you strain your muscles, throw out your back, or get hurt by a snapped shard. And the rock didn't even budge!

THE RIGHT WAY TO DO IT For jobs a shovel cannot do, use a pick. One end is chisel-shaped, while the other comes to a point. If all is in good condition and sharp, and swung properly, a pick will cut into hardpan. A pick can also wrap its curved point around a stubborn rock or buried root. Push hard to gain leverage for ejecting the obstruction.

For bigger jobs, try a crowbar, a long, slim steel rod with a wedge-shaped end. Lift it with both hands and swing hard, and it will plunge well into hard ground. Once maneuvered under a boulder or stump, get a block of wood or a small rock to create a fulcrum. This extra leverage will make all the difference.

For even larger jobs, particularly deeper roots or extensive, fibrous root systems, use a mattock, which is basically a heavy-duty pick with an ax-shaped head and a hoe-shaped end. The ax head, if swung directly and vigorously at the target, will slice through a root up to 4 inches thick.

IF I GOOFED, CAN I FIX IT? The longer you garden, or the more ambitious your yard projects become, the more you understand that you need a wide arsenal of tools. Invest in sturdy, well-made ones, and learn what to use when.

Buying the wrong kind of shovel

The most common and useful shovel for gardeners is the standard round-point model. The handle is usually fiberglass with a solid core or tight-grained ash; the round point allows easy penetration of a variety of materials; and the blade, assuming it has a strong dish, is stiff yet able to hold dirt well. It is generally the best tool for breaking new ground, digging, transplanting, lifting, and tossing.

It is the wrong tool for moving smaller plants; scooping lots of material; mixing concrete; digging trenches, drainage channels, or ditches; spreading gravel; loading; and doing other heavy-duty jobs. You'll know when you have the wrong shovel for the job. Your back—or your whole body—will protest, the blade will find no purchase or stuff will slide off the dish area, and the intended result will seem unattainable or a long, tortured way off.

THE RIGHT WAY TO DO IT Invest in a good-quality round-point shovel. Look for a solid socket whose head is made of a single forged and tempered piece of strong-gauge steel (the socket in the back will be closed, so there will be no hollow frog to clog with mud or dirt or weaken the blade). The handle material is your choice; improperly stored or cheap wooden ones split over time, but fiberglass might not be comfortable or to your taste. Shovels labeled "contractor grade" are always tougher, better made, and worth the extra money.

If you have a specialized project in mind, get a specialized shovel, following these guidelines for quality. Shop at a good farm-supply or hardware store for the best selection. A quick note about length: If your shovel doesn't provide the leverage you want, or your back is always aching, it could be that you don't need a different type, just one with a shorter or longer handle.

IF I GOOFED, CAN I FIX IT? Acknowledging that you have the wrong shovel for a job is easy. Getting the right one might be harder, but worth pursuing. If you don't know what you need or where to find it, ask around—consult other gardeners, do-it-yourselfers, or a professional landscaper, or find a well-stocked store with a staffer who knows the products.

Using dull tools

Dull tools are the harvest of ignorance or neglect. You use them, you wear them down, and you put them away (you might clean them beforehand, but you might not). Cheaply made, cheaply forged tools treated this way become pitted and rusty, and then wear out altogether—but not before they turn in lousy performances by gnawing, battering, tearing, or pulverizing their way through gardening projects. Well-made quality tools may forgive for a while, but in the end they too do unsatisfactory work and get ruined.

THE RIGHT WAY TO DO IT Dull edges make you work much harder, for much longer, to accomplish anything, souring even the sweetest task. A sharp, clean, maintained tool is a joy to use, working in concert to complete your digging, pruning, or planting project thoroughly, safely, neatly, and well.

The majority of gardening tools can be sharpened at home with a basic 10-inch file. Technically known as a mill bastard file, it has a single row of teeth cut diagonally across the file, adequate for all but the most seriously battered tools; bastard refers to its coarseness, the highest available is the 10-inch size. The object is to discover and restore the manufacturer's original bevel. Afterward, remove the feather, a thin strip of frail metal, which may have developed as you worked; do this with a light hand so you don't inadvertently create a double bevel. For some tools, such as a hoe, it is easier to do this work if you secure

it in a clamp. Hinged tools, like clippers and loppers, should be temporarily disassembled so you can file one blade without slicing your knuckles on the other.

If this is daunting, get someone who knows how to give you a lesson. Or take your tools to a professional sharpening service, such as at a mower-repair shop. It shouldn't be very expensive, and is well worth it.

IF I GOOFED, CAN I FIX IT? If you've ruined a tool with neglect and abuse and intend to replace it, vow to be kinder to the new one, especially if you decide to invest in a better-quality product. If you've tried to sharpen a tool and harmed it instead, take it to a professional sharpening service to see if it can be set right.

TREES

AVOID COMMON PROBLEMS WITH YOUR GARDEN'S BIGGEST CITIZENS.

Topping a tree

Cutting the top off, or removing a significant portion of a deciduous tree's topmost branches, is called topping. It is also known as pollarding, heading, stubbing, or dehorning. No matter what you call it, the object is to make a tree smaller and manage its growth. You might do it in an effort to control a wayward tree if it is expanding into space where you don't want it to be. You may also do this as a drastic form of pruning because the tree is spreading too much shade or shedding too many leaves or fruit.

Alas, topping doesn't work. A tree will respond by sending out a fresh burst of new growth and can catch up to its former size in just a few seasons. Meanwhile, your harsh surgery will provide an entryway for disease and pests and will invite decay, sunscald, and rot. Finally, removing a lot of topgrowth compromises a tree's ability to feed itself, as the leaves and branches you've eliminated can no longer conduct photosynthesis or contribute to the plant's health. The tree may start to starve, falter, and die.

THE RIGHT WAY TO DO IT If you want to control a tree's size and form, do smart and educated pruning throughout its life, not all at once. Take out dead and diseased branches, as well as those that are rubbing against each other, and then undertake some thinning (confine yourself to making moderate cuts over a period of years). If you think taking out a few major branches might work, consult an arborist. How much pruning a tree can handle in one season depends on what it is, how old it is, and whether it is healthy to begin with. If you are uncertain how to proceed, again, ask or hire a professional.

IF I GOOFED, CAN I FIX IT? Nope, sorry. A topped tree is a maimed, unhealthy, ugly tree. It will never look good again, even if you abstain from further cutting or bring in an arborist to clean up your work. Cut it down and open up the space for other, smaller plants, or replace it with a more modest-size tree.

Planting a tree too deeply

Planting a new, young tree is not difficult. You head to the local nursery in the spring and select a container-grown or bareroot plant. Its slender, stunted appearance should not discourage you; often, quite properly, it has been pruned back hard. Correctly planted and watered well, it won't be long before it starts to grow and expand.

If your new tree settles too deeply into the planting hole, or sinks or begins to lean somewhat in the days after planting—possibly because of the softness of the soil in the planting hole or because the water you've been diligently and correctly supplying has closed up air pockets, or both—you have a problem. If the trunk gets submerged too far belowground, roots will be deprived of necessary food, water, and air, and your new tree will struggle and maybe even perish. (If it's a dwarf fruit tree that's been grafted, the union should definitely not be buried.)

The same risk applies to balled-and-burlapped trees, which can be planted later in the gardening year. It is just as critical to not plant them too deeply, and trickier to maneuver or adjust them because their root balls are heavier.

THE RIGHT WAY TO DO IT Container-grown, bareroot, or balled-and-burlapped, the rule is the same. A tree must be planted at the same level as it was growing at the nursery, indicated by a line on the trunk (where the trunk ends and the roots begin). Sometimes the trunk will flare outward at this point—another way to gauge where the soil line should be. For containerized or bareroot trees, create a mound of soil in the hole's center and array the roots on it, adjusting the height until you are satisfied. (Some horticulturists claim you'll get more vigorous growth if you hose off the potting soil from the roots of container-grown trees before planting. If you do this, cover the roots with a damp cloth so they don't dry out.) For balled-and-burlapped ones, the hole size must be accurate, so invest extra effort in measuring the root ball and the cavity in which it will be planted. (As you create the hole, reserve fist-size chunks of sod, toss them back in when ready, get the root ball in, and remove chunks as needed.)

IF I GOOFED, CAN I FIX IT? Unfortunately, a sunken, sinking, or leaning tree will have to be carefully extracted and replanted at the correct depth. To minimize trauma, be extra gentle with the roots and keep them moist throughout the process.

Planting a tree too close to a structure

Trees get tall and broad over the years. This simple, inevitable fact may have escaped you years ago or eluded the last occupant of your home. Either way, size is now a problem. Certain branches, or entire trees, are rubbing against the house, porch, or deck, or a window, giving the area a crowded look. Or, worse, the tree is blocking sunlight, elbowing other plants into distorted growth, harming painted surfaces, siding, shingles, or the roof, or providing a bridge or haven for pests and insects.

THE RIGHT WAY TO DO IT In a perfect world, the gardener selecting a tree receives accurate information about the plant's mature size and takes this into account when placing it in the home landscape, giving it the space it will ultimately need. For fast-growing trees like Lombardy poplars or paulownia, you will soon see if you allowed enough space. For slow-growing trees, which include many evergreens, you need to believe what you've been told and allow room even though the tree may look lost or alone for a while. Give a tree good care, including sufficient water and maintenance pruning, so it will look its best. Don't fertilize, or overfertilize, if its mature size is a close fit.

IF I GOOFED, CAN I FIX IT? If the crowding has not become totally out of hand, some judicious pruning may solve the problem, at least for a while. However, do not cut excessively or recklessly in your desire to downsize a burgeoning plant, or you may create an eyesore. Find good pruning advice for your specific tree, or hire a professional arborist.

If a tree has truly outgrown its allotted spot, you can cut it down altogether or dig it up and move it to a better location. If you plan to replace it, be sure to do your homework so history doesn't repeat itself.

Amending the soil in the planting hole

Conventional wisdom about tree planting has changed over the years. Research has shown that if you amend the native soil with organic matter, such as compost, when you prepare a hole for a tree, you're not doing it any favors. The roots will be encouraged to circle around and stay in the hole, which is ultimately bad for the plant's stability and its overall health. This is especially true if the surrounding soil is heavy or compacted.

THE RIGHT WAY TO DO IT The current thinking is to encourage a tree to become well established in its home by amending the soil in the planting hole very little or not at all. It needs to become a native. (Preparing a planting bed for flowers or vegetables is a different matter, as those plants respond favorably to amended soil.)

There are two kinds of tree roots. Taproots vary from species to species in terms of how extensive (long) they become, but their purpose is twofold. They help anchor a tree in place, and they also avail themselves of groundwater, which helps the plant above survive when it is not watered regularly or there is a prolonged drought. Feeder roots, as their name implies, spread widely, but relatively shallowly, through the topsoil and upper layers of subsoil, absorbing water and nutrients.

Make a planting hole that's two to three times as wide as the tree's root ball, and use your shovel or a garden fork to scrape the insides and the bottom of the hole to loosen the surrounding soil. This encourages developing roots to venture outward and downward.

Mulch after planting to conserve soil moisture, moderate soil-temperature fluctuations, and keep encroaching weeds or grass at bay. Over time, it works its way down to improve soil texture and nourish the feeder roots. Be sure to replenish it occasionally. Keep mulch at least 6 inches away from the trunk, though, or the trunk may get too damp.

IF I GOOFED, CAN I FIX IT? Unless or until your tree shows signs of becoming root-bound (stunted growth, instability), it's probably too much trouble to try to fix this mistake. The worst-case scenario is the tree simply doesn't thrive and you ultimately have to move or replace it.

Not knowing whether to stake a tree

Professional arborists don't agree on whether a newly planted tree should be supported with stakes or guy wires. The need for support depends on the type of tree (fragile and slender baby fruit tree? probably wise; stout young spruce? maybe not) and the site (a very windy, open spot or one with light, sandy soil argues for support; a tight spot argues against it).

If you stake and you shouldn't have, you may find that your tree is not flexible in windy or stormy conditions. It may break rather than

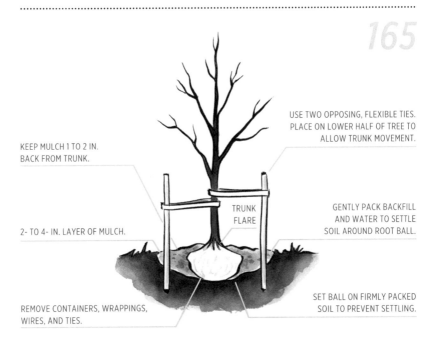

USE TWO OPPOSING, FLEXIBLE TIES.
PLACE ON LOWER HALF OF TREE TO
ALLOW TRUNK MOVEMENT.

KEEP MULCH 1 TO 2 IN.
BACK FROM TRUNK.

GENTLY PACK BACKFILL
AND WATER TO SETTLE
SOIL AROUND ROOT BALL.

TRUNK
FLARE

2- TO 4- IN. LAYER OF MULCH.

SET BALL ON FIRMLY PACKED
SOIL TO PREVENT SETTLING.

REMOVE CONTAINERS, WRAPPINGS,
WIRES, AND TIES.

bend. The materials you use to fasten the tree to the stake can also harm the bark and cause plant tissues to develop unevenly. If you stake incorrectly, the tree can grow larger above the tie than below it. Over time, it may lean away from the stake. Supporting a tree with guy wires is sometimes recommended for more mature, thicker-trunked trees (more than 4 inches in diameter), but carries similar risks.

THE RIGHT WAY TO DO IT Stake or support a newly planted tree with guy wires only if the nursery you bought it from specifically recommends you do so, or if you believe the planting site warrants it. Position single stakes on the upwind side of a tree. If you provide two or more stakes, or guy wires, for the sake of stability on a windy site or one with light or sandy soil, array them evenly around the tree (if only two, they should be perpendicular to the prevailing winds). Don't use ties that would abrade the bark; plastic tape, tubing, and the like is preferable to wire or string.

It is important not to leave supports in place too long, as a successful tree ultimately needs to be able to stand on its own. Remove supports once the roots establish themselves after a growing season.

IF I GOOFED, CAN I FIX IT? The sooner you notice your supports are being outgrown or doing more harm than good, the better. Remove them. If a tree has grown in the wrong direction, hopefully it will correct itself once unfettered. If the bark has become abraded, allow it to heal over.

Mishandling a wrapped root ball

Deciduous and evergreen trees are sold with a wrapped root ball. The plants are usually a few seasons old and field dug, and their root systems, along with some soil, are cinched up in a covering or wire cage. Assuming you pick a suitable spot and dig a good-size hole to receive this root system, handling such a tree requires great care. Do not pick it up by the trunk or stem, only by the ball. Handle the ball gingerly. The roots have already been pruned back before being wrapped up, so any further trauma or loss will be harmful.

Removing the covering, whether fabric or wire, before putting the tree in the hole may cause the entire root ball to fall apart or might seriously damage the remaining roots. Removing it after putting the tree in the hole is tricky and just as risky. A mishandled balled-and-burlapped tree can easily die soon after planting.

THE RIGHT WAY TO DO IT Buy only a freshly dug plant, which has the best chance for survival. Keep the root ball moist until planting time.

After you carefully maneuver the tree into its hole, remove any binding twine or wire. Next, test the covering by lighting a match to it. If it burns, it's fabric; if it melts, it's synthetic. If it's cloth, cut away as much as possible, and the rest will disintegrate. If it's synthetic, you will have to try to get it all off and out of there, using a combination of cutting and tugging.

It's hard to remove a wire basket without damaging the roots. Take off the top and any cinching wires, but don't tug or pull. Use wire cutters and remove in pieces. Most tree roots grow out to the sides, so if the covering is difficult to remove, give priority to getting rid of the top and as much of the sides as possible.

IF I GOOFED, CAN I FIX IT? You can scratch and dig your way at least partially back into the hole and undertake belated loosening or removal of the covering, then hope for the best. But don't even attempt this if the weather is hot and dry, or wintry and cold, as the stress will likely kill the tree.

VEGETABLES

GROW IN THE KNOW— AVOID COMMON ERRORS.

Crowding plants

No doubt about it, raising vegetables from seed is an act of faith. If you are new to it, or growing ones you have never tried before, you may not have enough faith. Whether you are bent over the seed flat or sowing seeds directly into the garden, you distribute more than you should. This is to hedge your bets in case there are a few duds.

Then all of them sprout. If you do nothing, they will crowd one another, jostling for space and resources and ultimately faltering or dying. So you thin. You yank out some, but others pull out at the same time, which was not your intention. Where to begin?

THE RIGHT WAY TO DO IT Ideally, don't sow too thickly to begin with. For indoor flats, if you are sowing larger seeds (like tomato or squash), handle them with your fingers and place them one at a time on the mix surface. If they are tiny seeds (like lettuce or radish), tap the open seed packet as you move it over the rows, back and forth, so they will roll out slowly. The goal is about ½ inch between seeds. When it comes time to thin (when the seeds have sprouted and developed their second set of leaves), it will be easier to pinch out unwanted ones carefully with your fingertips, or snip them with a pair of manicure or small sewing scissors.

Outdoors, put down two or three seeds together, then move on down the row, sowing at the spacing recommended on the seed packet. Thin to the strongest seedling once they have developed their second set of leaves. This works well for corn and beans, among others. Do not be sentimental—be ruthless. If you do not thin properly, nobody wins.

IF I GOOFED, CAN I FIX IT? It depends on how thickly you've sowed. If you are very careful and patient, you may be able to thin to one strong seedling at the recommended intervals. If you have an impenetrable thicket on your hands, admit your mistake and start over.

Setting out tender crops too early

Call it a rookie mistake, or being overeager, or just plain bad luck, but putting certain vegetable seedlings into the ground too soon can lead to their demise. The more tender warm-weather vegetables (corn, tomatoes, peppers, and eggplants) don't do well in cold, sodden ground. They'll rot, or at best sulk and grow poorly, if set out too early in the spring. Or a late frost can flatten or blacken and kill them overnight. When this happens, you have to start all over again—a setback made all the more disappointing by your wasted time, resources, and effort.

THE RIGHT WAY TO DO IT Wait until the weather and soil have warmed up and all danger of frost is past. Then, just to be certain, check the soil consistency. It's safe for planting when a ball gathered in your hand falls apart when you poke it with a finger. Regarding soil temperature, gardening expert Roger B. Swain provides this simple, apt guideline: "I try not to plant seed in soil that I wouldn't be comfortable lying down in."

If the seedlings you've raised indoors or recently purchased seem to be outgrowing their flats and it's not time yet, carefully transplant them into larger or individual pots. If they're getting lanky or leaning toward the light, move them closer to a light source (lower your grow light or raise their shelf, or set them in a window and give them a quarter turn each day). If your frost-free date is two weeks away or less, start hardening off the tender seedlings so they will move more readily into the garden. Bring them outside during the day to a sheltered area, such as a porch or under a big tree, and remember to bring them in at night. This practice makes a big difference.

IF I GOOFED, CAN I FIX IT? There are tricks for helping tender seedlings tolerate cold or frosty weather, assuming they are still alive after being exposed. Carefully shield them at night with row covers, plastic or glass cloches, cardboard boxes, or a Wall O'Water. A nice, fluffy mulch several inches thick around them also helps, as will providing consistent and adequate water. A way around this entire issue is to create raised beds for your vegetable garden. These warm up earlier in spring and drain away excess water faster, too.

172

Planting cool-weather crops too late

Although spring weather is not always predictable and plants are generally forgiving, you can damage a plant's chances by putting it in the garden at the wrong time. Cool-weather crops (radish, broccoli, cauliflower, Brussels sprouts, and lettuce, spinach, and other salad greens) really do perform better in the shorter days of spring (and fall, in many areas). Summer-warmed soil, plus long, hot sunny days, can result in a poor show, as the warmth inspires them to bolt. A central or several center flower stalks quickly shoot up, bloom, and go to seed. At that point, the plant has ceased to put any energy into the edible parts you'd hoped to enjoy, and the opportunity for a good, tasty harvest is over (leaves of bolted lettuce, for example, taste bitter).

THE RIGHT WAY TO DO IT Choose varieties labeled bolt-resistant. If you raise your own seedlings, read and follow the suggested timetable on the seed packets so you get them started early enough indoors and they will be ready to move into the garden on schedule. If you get them started too late—or buy leftovers at your local garden center— they will go into the ground too late.

A couple of other tricks can prevent bolting. Don't use row covers or cloches that hold in too much warmth. Minimize stress, such as by watering consistently so they are evenly moist and don't experience extremes. For lettuce, you can pick off (and eat) outer leaves so younger ones keep getting produced. Finally, because this entire process is admittedly unpredictable, it's wise to make successive sowings every two weeks or so. Somewhere in there you will be able to pick a fine harvest.

IF I GOOFED, CAN I FIX IT? Plants that are bolting or bolted cannot be brought back to a harvestable state, so tear them out and toss them on your compost pile. You might also seek out varieties that sprout, grow, and fruit faster, such as short-season ones that naturally avoid the hotter weather.

Trying to grow vegetables in too little sun

Most vegetable crops are sun lovers: they need at least six hours a day of full sun. You may get so caught up in the fact that you have what appears to be an ideal spot—mostly level, well-drained ground, out in the open—that you forget to check for this key requirement.

Unfortunately, there is no way to cheat. Limited light and ground that isn't sun-warmed do not make a recipe for successful vegetable growth. At best, the plants will grow slowly or lean toward the direction of the most sunlight. At worst, they won't produce many, or any, blossoms, just leaves.

THE RIGHT WAY TO DO IT Before you even create a new vegetable garden, rope off or otherwise mark the intended outline and observe it morning, noon, and evening to verify that it gets at least six hours of daily sun. It's best to orient a garden so the rows run east to west. You can put the tallest plants (such as bean teepees) on the north end so they won't shade the shorter ones.

IF I GOOFED, CAN I FIX IT? Observe the garden during various times of day. If a shade source can be eliminated (take down that tree) or diminished (move the shed, prune nearby trees and shrubs), do so.

174

If there is no realistic way to get more sunlight into the spot, move the vegetable garden to a more suitable site, whether it's a slight adjustment or all the way across the yard.

WHAT ELSE?

Vegetables that put forth only leaves and little or no edible fruit may also be suffering from dehydration (water more often and more thoroughly), poor nutrition (was the soil amended before planting? do you fertilize with the right plant food for vegetable crops?), or frost damage (cold air can kill off buds and developing flowers), just to name a few. Check and correct for these conditions.

Accidentally killing good bugs

Finding bugs in your garden can be disconcerting, especially because they may be dining on your plants. If you assume the worst and spray or dust with an insecticide, you may succeed in killing or at least discouraging them. But you may also be sorry. Some insects should be welcome in our gardens, either because they are not harmful (pollinating bees) or because they prey on bad bugs (ladybugs devour aphids). A knee-jerk reaction of alarm and assault can upset the balance of your little ecosystem.

THE RIGHT WAY TO DO IT Even before you attempt to put a name to the bug you are concerned about, observe it. What is it actually doing in your garden—eating, nesting, hunting, burrowing, collecting pollen, nibbling

on honeydew, spinning a web? Also, try to figure out how many you have—is it a few or an infestation? This will help you decide how to act.

It may be that the bug you see is one of the so-called beneficial insects, such as ladybugs, lacewings, parasitic wasps, honeybees, flower flies, spiders, and predaceous ground beetles. Even yellow jackets fall into this category, as adults gather other insects to feed to their growing larvae.

When applying any garden pesticide, always read the label to see if it might be harmful to beneficial insects you have seen in your garden, then weigh the risks before using. For example, Bt (*Bacillus thuringiensis*) kills butterfly larvae as well as pest caterpillars, and sabadilla dust harms honeybees. Insecticides with an active ingredient of pyrethrum or rotenone are toxic to all insects (organic gardeners do not use them on food crops).

You might also look into companion planting (for example, fennel and dill both attract a beneficial wasp that preys on aphids).

IF I GOOFED, CAN I FIX IT? The best penance for applying a pesticide that kills more than the intended target is to stop using it immediately and allow your garden to rebound if it can. Educate yourself on pest controls and their risks.

176

Making your vegetable garden too big (or too small)

If this is your first time vegetable gardening and you start out full of eagerness, energy, and ambition, it's easy to overestimate or underestimate. It's dispiriting when you realize the project is awfully time-consuming, what with constant watering, weeding, thinning, and picking, not to mention contending with possible pests (animal and insect) and finding uses for big harvests. Your vegetable garden is too big, and you're not having fun. In fact, you're a bit overwhelmed.

Or maybe you are the cautious type, and installed a too-small vegetable patch. The plants are jammed in, and it's tricky to water, weed, and harvest. Or the plants are not as productive as you had hoped, either because they are crowded or you simply didn't plant enough.

THE RIGHT WAY TO DO IT Coming up with the right size vegetable garden starts with careful forethought before you break ground, order seeds, or buy a single plant. Make a plan on paper, to scale (use graph paper if you like). It's much easier to add and delete plants, widen the patch, create a path down the middle, and so on, when it's only on paper.

To determine how much space to allow individual plants, find out—in general terms, as results will vary from garden to garden—what the expected mature size will be. Get this information from the back of the seed packet, in the seed company's catalog or on its website, or in reference books. Draw, shift, add, subtract, and dream. When you're satisfied with your plan, implement it. Keep a garden notebook or take photos so you can fine-tune it the following year.

IF I GOOFED, CAN I FIX IT? A too-small garden can be enlarged, and a too-big one can be scaled back, using what you've learned about vegetables and about yourself as a vegetable gardener. Again, plan the modified garden on paper first. If it's an expansion, do the extra digging or create the additional raised bed(s) in the fall so there's less work facing you next spring. If it's a reduction, fall is also a good time to sow grass seed, install low-maintenance plants, or lay down stones.

VINES
ACHIEVE THE COVERAGE AND LOOK YOU ENVISION

Letting wisteria get out of hand

When a wisteria is well established and blooming lustily, there are few plants as spectacular and seemingly easy. But when this vine causes you trouble, boy, does it ever. The most common complaint about wisteria, whether it's a young plant or one that's been around for years, is that it simply won't bloom. Maybe you pruned it at the wrong time (spring is inadvisable because wisteria blooms on last year's growth), or you have insufficient sunlight. However, moving a wisteria plant to a sunnier spot is a big project. The vining stems may be extensive and the root system is imposing and difficult to dig up. You could end up setting back or even killing the plant.

Wisteria is legendary for its rampant growth, particularly in warmer areas. It can strangle a tree, insinuate itself into shingles, and lift a roof.

180

Pruning too timidly or just letting it go can cause the situation to get out of control.

THE RIGHT WAY TO DO IT Try nudging your reluctant wisteria: feed and water it regularly during the spring and summer, and stake or tie it as needed. Remove suckers at the base, which steal energy that could be put into blooming. A drastic, but often effective, measure is summer root pruning. Using a sharp spade, slice the roots in a 2-foot radius from the main stem. Then create a shallow trench and fill it with soil mixed with a good dose of superphosphate (up to 4 pounds for each inch of trunk diameter), and water well. This should jolt the plant into sending energy into blooming stems.

To control rampant growth, prune in late spring or early summer, immediately after blooming. Cut back the shoots at about the seventh leaf. You can also partially cut back unruly, too-long growth at this time.

IF I GOOFED, CAN I FIX IT? If your wisteria is not blooming, perhaps you just need to be patient. Large, well-established plants bloom best, and sometimes the wait can be 15 years or more.

If your wisteria is a house eater and you've neglected, or attempted and failed at, control, it may be time to cut it all the way back, or even to kill it and consider a more demure replacement vine.

Planting clematis too shallowly

You would never guess from looking at an older, robust clematis vine that it's something of a tender creature. Not in terms of cold-hardiness—most do fine in Zones 5 to 9, and some can survive as far

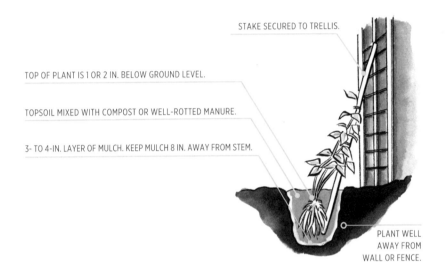

STAKE SECURED TO TRELLIS.

TOP OF PLANT IS 1 OR 2 IN. BELOW GROUND LEVEL.

TOPSOIL MIXED WITH COMPOST OR WELL-ROTTED MANURE.

3- TO 4-IN. LAYER OF MULCH. KEEP MULCH 8 IN. AWAY FROM STEM.

PLANT WELL AWAY FROM WALL OR FENCE.

north as Zone 3—but rather in terms of getting off to a good start. Proper siting and planting are key. Clematis like cool roots, yet the vine itself is happy to clamber aloft into the sunshine. If the roots are exposed and subjected to dry soil and hot sun, the plant struggles and dies. Clematis also prefers somewhat alkaline soil, and if placed in ground that is too acidic, it will sulk, producing spindly foliage and few blooms.

Clematis should not be planted too shallowly, partly because a young plant might topple over before it establishes a good relationship with its support (a trellis, sturdy netting, or a network of wires and eyebolts on a wall). Furthermore, if the topgrowth is damaged during the growing season or over a hard winter, the roots cannot regroup and send out new growth.

THE RIGHT WAY TO DO IT Plant a bareroot clematis in early spring, while it is still dormant. (Container-grown ones, available later in the season, may be planted afterward.) Pick a suitable spot and prepare the hole well, adding organic matter and perhaps a sprinkle of lime.

Look for the crown, the place where the stem meets the roots. Submerge the crown 1 or 2 inches below the soil surface. It will form roots as the plant establishes itself and will be stabler—plus, as mentioned, more resilient. Mulch, water well and frequently, and be patient. Clematis vines usually take at least two seasons to reach their stride.

IF I GOOFED, CAN I FIX IT? If you realize your error soon after planting, replant. Do it right and handle the plant very gently. If it's been many weeks, a season, or even an entire year since you planted your clematis too shallowly, you already know the plant is unhappy. If it still has life in it, you can try replanting correctly. Otherwise, tear it out and start again with a new one.

Failing to give a vine proper support

Not supporting a vine at all—simply planting it near something you hope it will ascend—doesn't work well. Even one with clinging tendrils (such as passionflower vine, *Passiflora caerulea*) can wander in the wrong direction, sprawl, or get itself into a tangle. At the very least, you should provide a guiding string or wire to encourage it in the right direction. Insufficient support is also bad. A slender wooden trellis, for example, will surely fail a lush grower such as a black-eyed Susan vine (*Thunbergia alata*), a trumpet flower (*Campsis radicans*), or even a vining tomato plant. The plant's weight and rangy growth will soon exceed the slats, and the trellis will lean to one side and may eject from the ground altogether. Meanwhile, the stems will take off in odd directions or bend and break.

THE RIGHT WAY TO DO IT To pair a vine with the right support, plan for its projected mature size. Don't be fooled by the small or frail seedling you bring home in a gallon pot. True, pruning can rein in rampant growth, and training can guide branches, but an appropriate initial match is key. Use quality, sturdy materials, and overestimate. You and your vine will live to regret the choice of something too short, narrow, brittle, or flimsy. Also, attend to stability—sink a support deeply into the ground. A foot and a half to two feet down is not excessive.

IF I GOOFED, CAN I FIX IT? It's often possible to cinch or reroute a vine belatedly, but the plant may get in your way as you work, you may inadvertently damage it, and it won't look great. Inserting more substantial support for a vine once it's big also runs the risk of damaging the root system as you try to plunge it into the ground deeply enough. When a vine has become unwieldy, you can surrender for the season and chop it back in the fall or early spring, resolving to provide better support in the coming years. Hopefully the plant will rebound and look great in the future.

184

Pruning or cutting back at the wrong time

There are all sorts of reasons to prune a vine: it's getting too tall or wide; it's encroaching on nearby plants; it's taxing its support's ability to hold it up; it's rambling in the wrong directions; it has straggly or unproductive branches; or it's reached a point where most growth, including flowers, are out of reach or out of sight. Without pruning, many vines become unruly and crowded, which is neither attractive nor healthy.

You can harm healthy vine growth by removing, redirecting, and grooming it at the wrong time. Prune in the fall, and your cuts may inspire a fresh flush of growth that the cold weather then damages. Pruning when a vine is lush, in late spring or in early summer, can lead to chopping off next season's flower buds.

THE RIGHT WAY TO DO IT You can take out dead, diseased, storm- or insect-damaged, weak, and old-wood stems without harming your vine—after all, they are never going to recover. You can do so at practically any time, but late winter or early spring is best, while the plant is still dormant, because you can see the plant's profile better when it is not full of leafy growth.

Most perennial vines bloom on wood that grew the previous year. You may prune to shape the plant, thin it out, or control growth immediately after the flowers fade and before the plant starts forming buds for next year's show. One especially tricky vine is clematis, because some flower on current-season growth and some do not. Correctly identify your species, then track down the necessary information at a nursery or in a good book on pruning.

Generally speaking, any growing-season pruning should be light and judicious. If you have a very rampant and aggressive vine (say, trumpet creeper, akebia, or ivy), you may chop it back in late winter or early spring while it is still dormant; regrowth will occur soon after.

IF I GOOFED, CAN I FIX IT? If you pruned a vine too zealously or at the wrong time of year, give it at least one growing season to recover.

Using the wrong vine

If you choose a vine simply because it is attractive, then plunk it in (while providing support), you may soon regret your hasty decision. If it's a sun lover and doesn't get enough light, its coverage will be sparse and it may not flower or fruit well, or at all. If it's an aggressive plant, it may pull down or overwhelm its support in a few seasons. You may get tired of perpetually chopping it back, or you may not want to bother. If it's a naturally delicate grower, you may never get the coverage you wanted.

THE RIGHT WAY TO DO IT Make a good match between the vine and the place in which you want it to grow. If you do some research (online, in gardening books and magazines, or simply by lingering at the garden center reading labels and asking questions), you may be pleasantly surprised at the range of choices.

Ivy, Virginia creeper, or wintercreeper (*Euonymus*) can provide thick screening coverage for a wall or a fence. For a sturdy arch or pergola, try a climbing rose, kiwi, wisteria, or bougainvillea. Trumpet flower, black-eyed Susan vine, morning glory (an annual that must be replanted each spring) all produce plentiful flowers. For informal coverage of an eyesore, jasmine and honeysuckle are good choices. Ivy and hops will do if you need fast, leafy coverage. For elegant form and color, clematis is queen. For draping a strong tree, climbing hydrangea, wisteria, and some climbing roses, with training, will do a glorious job.

IF I GOOFED, CAN I FIX IT? You may be confronted with a choice: the support or the vine. If the support is an important part of your yard (such as a pergola or archway), tear out the problematic vine and replace it with something more suitable. If you really like a certain vine, you can change its support, preferably in late winter or early spring when the plant is dormant or growing slowly and won't mind being cut back or jostled.

WATERING

WATERING WISDOM LEADS TO LESS WORK AND BETTER PLANTS.

Overwatering

You left the sprinkler or irrigation system on too long. Or your watering system is on a timer and ran when the weather was already wet. Or you or someone else, in a well-intentioned effort to nurture the lawn, flowerbed, or vegetable garden, poured on entirely too much water. If you don't notice all the excess water running off, the plants will soon clue you in. Sodden soil and the resulting lack of oxygen cause roots to rot, stems to turn squishy and flaccid, and leaves to yellow. Collapse and death often follow. Whether because of neglect, inattentiveness, or overzealousness, overwatering can kill.

THE RIGHT WAY TO DO IT The key to giving your lawn and garden enough—but not too much—water is to be attentive. Rainfall can be capricious or unpredictable, and your soil type and plants have unique qualities and synergy. Routine, rote watering (using a timer, or watering the same amount every time) is risky.

Before you can get your garden on a watering schedule, you need to observe and fine-tune, and you must remain alert and poised to intervene if it looks like your routine is leading to overwatering. Most yards use about 1 inch of water every week (more in quick-draining or dry conditions, less in clay-heavy soil or humid weather). There are ways to measure how much you are delivering, notably the simple method of setting out tin cans while watering, then checking how much they collect. You can also dig down around your plants after watering to see how deeply the moisture has sunk in. Simpler still, though less precise, is to watch the plants for signs that they are getting too much water.

IF I GOOFED, CAN I FIX IT? The sooner you notice you've delivered too much water, the better. Let it drain away (aided with ad hoc trenches, if need be) and allow the area to dry out. Assess the surviving plants and chop back or discard those that were harmed.

Overlooking poor drainage

Water is critical to plants' survival, but achieving a good balance can be difficult. Don't assume that the plant's soil will automatically shed or drain away any excess, whether it's a good soaking out in the garden or a saturated potted plant. If your garden soil drains poorly, which is often the case with soils that are high in clay or beds in low spots, the water will just puddle around the plants. Waterlogged soil deprives roots of needed oxygen, and they will soon drown and rot. Aboveground, the stems and even the crown of the plant (the point where it meets the soil) will also rot. You'll see the same thing in an overwatered potted plant, when the soil mix is too heavy or the container lacks drainage holes.

THE RIGHT WAY TO DO IT Ideally, assess the situation before planting anything. Observe the site to see whether there is puddling or poor drainage, confirm your suspicions by digging down several inches, and correct it accordingly.

You can improve poor drainage by digging in organic matter, which improves the soil texture and helps unneeded water to drain away. Or you may need to create a gully or drainage ditch that diverts incoming water away from the planting bed (possibly filling it with gravel). You can correct severe drainage problems with more sophisticated measures, including installing underground perforated pipes, although you might need to hire a professional for this job. Alternatively, you could either abandon the idea of planting a soggy spot or landscape it with plants known to relish such conditions (for example, many irises do beautifully in such conditions).

IF I GOOFED, CAN I FIX IT? Many garden plants will not survive for long when subjected to soil that is too wet. They can expire in a matter of a day or days, and there's nothing to do but tear them out, rotten root systems and all. But if a plant is still alive or revives when wet weather subsides, take corrective measures. Improve the drainage as described, or move the beleaguered plant to a more suitable spot.

Watering too lightly

Watering the garden takes time and patience. You may stand there with the hose for a while, sprinkling an area before moving on to the next one, and think you've done a good job. But if you were to dig down with a trowel, you might be surprised to find that the water did not soak in to the depth of 6 or more inches that the root systems of most flowers and vegetables require. Shallow-rooted lawn grass manages with a bit less, and roses and shrubs relish deeper drenchings.

Plant roots respond to insufficient water by staying near or growing up closer to the surface. Small newly introduced plants are especially vulnerable. When warm sunshine quickly dries out the upper layers of the soil, these shallow, thirsty roots dry out. The result? Aborted blossoms, fallen petals, poor fruit development, and stunted growth, followed by wilting, drooping, dying, and eventually dead plants.

THE RIGHT WAY TO DO IT Deep, infrequent soakings are so much better than shallow, frequent sprinklings. The roots will develop and grow downward to access that water, and become stronger and more drought-resistant as a result. Wherever possible, create basins around individual plants so water goes into and stays in the intended area. Fill a basin, and move on to the next, then double back and repeat if necessary. (As mentioned, you can check how deeply the water has soaked in by plunging in a trowel and having a look.) Run the water slowly but steadily and it will soak in better. Finally, mulch helps retain soil moisture and prevent evaporation.

IF I GOOFED, CAN I FIX IT? Plants can certainly develop deeper root systems and become more resilient and healthier. Start watering them more deeply and less frequently.

WHAT ELSE?

A wilting plant is not always a thirsty plant. On a very dry day with low humidity, the plant simply may not be able to deliver water to its leaves fast enough, even though its soil area is sufficiently moistened. Check the soil before rushing in with extra water. If you think this is the problem, break the usual rule and sprinkle or mist the leaves.

Watering the leaves

A common error is watering a plant's leaves rather than delivering water directly to its root system. The water runs and drips down to where it needs to be, more or less, but some evaporates and some will run off.

Watering a plant the wrong way is not merely inefficient; the practice can have serious consequences for plant health. Damp leaves, especially those that are moist late in the day or through the night, become susceptible to disfiguring fungal diseases. For example, wet leaves on your rosebushes are vulnerable to downy mildew; wet leaves on a hollyhock are prone to rust. Also, if you prune, groom, or harvest damp plants and a few of them are already diseased, you may unintentionally spread the problem (blight, leaf-spot mildew) to others.

THE RIGHT WAY TO DO IT It's not only beneficial to water your plants at ground level; it's more efficient and usually easier. Either lay the hose at the base of a plant or grouping and let the water trickle in slowly, thread a soaker hose throughout a flowerbed or vegetable patch, use a watering wand with a gentle rose head, or invest in a drip-irrigation system. No matter how you deliver water, remember that a gentle, slow flow always soaks in best. A strong blast from the hose only dislodges soil, mulch, and sometimes the plants themselves.

Finally, tailor the amount of water you deliver to the type of soil you have. Clay soil needs to be watered quite slowly and less often than a good loam, while sandy soil drains quickly and needs more frequent, deeper watering. Where possible, add organic matter (well-rotted compost is ideal) to such soils in an effort to bring them closer to the happy medium of loam.

IF I GOOFED, CAN I FIX IT? Change the way you water, the method and speed of delivery, and perhaps even the time of day you water. Good watering habits will result in healthier, happier plants—and, as a bonus, you will probably lower your water bill.

Using the wrong watering tools

Thoughtless watering, coupled with using the wrong device, doesn't do your plants any favors. If you use sprinklers for everything in your yard, you are going to get mixed results when the water misses some of its intended targets and runs off. Plus, leaves are getting damp, which is not good. Direct hose blasts just lead to wasteful runoff, and they dislodge soil, mulch, or even the plant itself—plus, it's difficult to water at the correct duration. Watering cans require frequent trips to a spigot and are a labor-intensive way to irrigate distant parts of the garden or especially thirsty plants.

THE RIGHT WAY TO DO IT Treat yourself, and your garden plants, to the great pleasure of using the right tool for each watering job. Take a trip to a well-stocked garden center or hardware store, or go to a garden-supply website to feast your eyes and educate yourself about the many options. Select a quality hose that doesn't kink, then check out accessories. Wands are wonderful for delivering a gentle but drenching spray to the base of rosebushes, to overhead hanging baskets, to windowboxes, to newly planted perennials and shrubs, and more. Get one with a thumb-operated shut-off valve. Nozzles, with triggers that allow you to regulate the intensity of the spray, are worth the invest-ment for targeted watering. As for sprinklers, the classic whirlybird remains a fine choice for lawns as well as for delivering water to a large vegetable garden or a home orchard. So-called sled sprinklers (rotating or impulse) are easy to drag to a new spot while the water is still running. Oscillating sprinklers, which also attach to a hose, are excellent for larger lawns or groundcover areas.

These more modern innovations have not necessarily made the good old watering can obsolete. It's still an effective way to gently water potted or young plants or to deliver water-soluble fertilizer to specific plants.

IF I GOOFED, CAN I FIX IT? Noticing that your watering method is poor or inefficient is the first step. Go shopping for new and better watering tools.

WEEDS AND PROBLEM PLANTS

COMBAT, OUTWIT, OR ERADICATE UNWANTED PLANTS.

Letting weeds go to seed

Being slow to act, or not acting at all, can lead to a weed-population explosion, and it's all too easy to learn this the hard way. Here are a couple of scary statistics: one lamb's-quarters plant (*Chenopodium album*) can generate up to 70,000 seeds; a single dandelion (*Taraxacum officinale*) puffball can send forth between 100 and 400 seeds. Granted, not all of these will successfully germinate, but knowing this underscores the need to control common weeds before they disperse their bounty and you have an infestation that's increasingly difficult to eradicate.

Delaying intervention while the plants grow, but have not yet flowered, is bad for your garden. Such impressive fertility requires a lot of energy, and young weeds will suck up moisture and nutrients that your less-aggressive, desirable garden plants will not get.

THE RIGHT WAY TO DO IT The earlier you fight back, the better. Young weeds that have not yet formed flowers, or at least have not gone to seed, are easier to kill or discourage, whether by closely mowing them, knocking them down with a sharp hoe, digging them out, or even applying an herbicide. It's easier to yank or dig them out of damp ground after a rain (but before they start using that welcome drink to generate a growth surge).

Be vigilant almost year-round. Some weeds are annuals (they jump up in the spring and rush to flower, and produce those unwelcome seeds, in one growing season), some are winter annuals (they germinate in the fall, overwinter, and bloom in the spring), and some are biennials (they flower and seed in their second season).

IF I GOOFED, CAN I FIX IT? Take action—the sooner, the better, before the infestation grows exponentially. If weeds are overtaking your lawn, consult a lawn service about your options and weigh whether you will use herbicides, which can have a negative impact on the environment. If weeds have invaded a flowerbed or overrun a vegetable garden, you may have to tear out everything—even the good plants—and take the area out of commission while you smother or poison as many of the weed seeds as possible.

Planting a garden thug

You didn't know, or you got lulled. That gooseneck loosestrife (*Lysimachia clethroides*), creeping Jenny (*Lysimachia nummularia*), cypress spurge (*Euphorbia cyparissias*), or shamrock (*Oxalis* species) looked so appealing in the gardening book or magazine or at the garden center. At first you were pleased with how well it took to life in your yard. It showed little trauma from transplanting and put out new growth in short order—and then more new growth, and more, and more. At this point, clipping back its runners or tearing out unwelcome roots and offspring aren't really controlling its spread.

THE RIGHT WAY TO DO IT

Always beware of plants that are described as "vigorous," "resilient," or even "trouble-free," which likely means they are rampant, difficult to kill, and completely independent. Also check the growing requirements, as a number of plants said to prefer damp ground become invasive when your garden provides all the moisture they need. The same plants might be more circumspect in drier soil or with less water, or may be better enjoyed in a pot or planter.

IF I GOOFED, CAN I FIX IT? If a desirable or ornamental plant is already running amok, there are various ways to rein it in or confine it, such as installing a border around its growing area (including sinking barriers well into the ground so roots and runners cannot breach it), cutting off runners at the plant's crown, and removing all flowers before they can go to seed. If you really want to kill the pest, try smothering the patch by placing boards, a thick layer of straw, or anchored black plastic over it, mowing down the plants over and over again from the moment they emerge in spring and all through the growing season, or undertaking a thorough digging-up operation. As a last resort, carefully deploy an herbicide.

Growing toxic plants

Some garden plants are poisonous. Garden centers don't always post warnings, so you might have no way of knowing a plant is toxic until someone falls sick. While it's rare for a child or pet to eat leaves, berries, seedpods, or roots, it can happen, and the worst-case scenario is grim.

Among the common plants that should never be ingested are rhubarb (very poisonous leaves), larkspur (seedlings as well as seeds), monkshood (roots), irises (rhizomes), daphne (berries), castor bean (even one seed can be lethal), yew (berries and needles), oleander (leaves, stems), daffodils (bulbs), and all parts of rhododendrons, azaleas, and cherry laurels. Symptoms vary depending on the plant and the size of the person or animal ingesting it, but they can range from digestive upset to irregular heartbeat to fatal seizures.

THE RIGHT WAY TO DO IT If small children or unleashed pets frequently visit your yard, err on the side of caution and supervise them at all times. Lecture children from the time they can understand to never, ever ingest anything in the garden. Never let them see you sampling anything, which could awaken their curiosity or give them a false sense of security.

When shopping for plants, inquire about their safety or look it up yourself. If you choose something that is potentially harmful, block direct access to it with other plants or garden decor (plant in the back of a flowerbed), trim off low branches, or even post a warning sign.

IF I GOOFED, CAN I FIX IT? Chances are if a child or pet manages to consume and get sick from a daffodil bulb or the yew bush in your

yard, you'll be inclined to tear it out and replace it with something safe. If you opt to keep it, employ at least one of the safety measures described.

If you ever suspect poisoning, immediately call for help—911 for a person, and the nearest vet for a pet. (Find a list of plants toxic to pets at aspca.org/pet-care/poison-control/plants.) Also, be sure to get a sample of the plant you suspect caused the problem; anyone treating the afflicted person or animal will want it.

Leaving exposed, open ground

Ah, the clean slate. You've laid out and dug up the new flowerbed or vegetable patch—pulled all the weeds, dug out roots and rocks, and raked it neatly. But in an amazingly short time, the area fills with unwelcome weeds. They didn't just blow in there, though. The cultivating and raking brought them forth, and exposure to air, sunlight, and water right at or near the soil surface gave them all they needed to germinate. If you tolerate their presence too long, not only will they be hard to beat back, but they will also start to negatively affect your flowers (stunting growth or reducing flowering) or crops (yields will drop).

THE RIGHT WAY TO DO IT It's impossible to avoid bringing dormant weed seeds to the surface when you cultivate new ground. The trick is to discourage them before they can start absorbing the water and nutrients you want to keep available to the plants you install. You have a window of two to three weeks before it becomes a losing fight.

Attack fields of tiny, just-germinated weeds with a sharp hoe. Wield your weapon shallowly, however, so you don't stir up still more weed seeds or harm the roots of your desirable plants. Then, or alternatively, lay down a smothering mulch (2 or more inches thick), which cuts off light to the weed seedlings, over all open spots. The mulch will also be beneficial for the desired plants, moderating soil-temperature fluctuations and helping retain soil moisture so you don't have to water as often. Replenish the mulch as needed.

IF I GOOFED, CAN I FIX IT? If there's a carpet of weed seedlings in a new bed, and you haven't yet planted anything there, delay planting and do battle. Lay a thick mulch, 2 or 3 inches deep, over the entire area. Or cover the bed with black plastic or a tarp, anchoring the edges. Either way, leave the covering securely in place for several weeks, checking occasionally to see if the seedlings have expired. Plant, and mulch to discourage them from returning.

Planting the groundcover from hell

Some groundcovers turn out to be a complete hassle. Either their coverage is too sparse and weeds invade (and how do you kill the weeds without harming the groundcover?) or the plants turn out to be overly aggressive and start invading your lawn or flowerbeds. Either way, it's clear that the groundcover from hell has turned out to be more of a problem than a solution.

THE RIGHT WAY TO DO IT First, pick your plant wisely. Make sure it is a fair match for the site (sun or shade, or partial shade; dry or damp ground; acidic or alkaline soil). Next, prepare the area by digging out existing plants, including weeds, removing obstructions like rocks and roots, and improving the soil with organic matter. If you already know your chosen plant is on the invasive side, install boundaries, such as a trench all the way around the area or edging material sunk down well into the ground, to thwart root and runner expansion.

When planting, allow for future growth by spacing the seedlings at equal intervals, either in rows or in a checkerboard or staggered pattern. Create little basins around each plant to make water delivery more efficient. Now, mulch. Use straw, pine needles, bark mulch, or even pebbles, and cover over all of the open areas. Keep an eye on this mulch as the season progresses, yanking out weeds and renewing as needed. Yes, hand-pulling remains the best way to keep weeds out of your groundcover. In time, the little plants will fill in the area, shading out developing weeds and creating the carpet you originally envisioned.

IF I GOOFED, CAN I FIX IT? If your groundcover becomes infested with weeds too numerous to hand pull, or the infestation turns out to be an aggressive pest, you have no option but to kill it, and hopefully start over. Try mowing it down and smothering it with an extra-deep layer of mulch (or mulch on top of several layers of newspaper). This can be just as effective as blasting it with an herbicide, and it has less impact on the environment.

Letting perennial weeds take hold

Not all weeds are created equal, and perennial weeds can be daunting adversaries once they get a foothold in your yard and garden. Even if you are watchful and cut them down with a hoe, like you do with sprouting annual weeds, they can still get the upper hand. Generally speaking, their main modes of reproduction are their root systems (ground ivy) and prolific production of runners (quack grass). When you try to dig them up, if you leave any portion of root or runner behind, they can and will return. Tilling an affected area can actually make the weed problem worse by distributing chopped-up bits throughout the bed, each capable of regenerating. It sounds like a science-fiction nightmare, but it is all too real.

THE RIGHT WAY TO DO IT First, to correctly identify a weed as a perennial type, look it up or show a sample to someone knowledgeable. Or simply take your cue from the fact that your enemy clearly has extensive, deep, vigorous root systems.

Ideally, start combating perennial weeds when they are still small in size and number. Mulch thickly or cover a bed with plastic. For weeds that get through these barriers, go after them with a sharp hoe or by hand pulling or spot treating with an herbicide. Do not till or hoe deeply, and work to extract the entire root system (which is much more easily accomplished when the ground is damp). A garden fork is a better tool for digging out extended plants (a shovel or trowel tends to just break the roots).

IF I GOOFED, CAN I FIX IT? Once you have identified their presence, do not allow perennial weeds to spread, or the problem will only get worse. In moderate cases, apply diligent, consistent combat as described. Depending on which weed you are fighting and how much of a foothold it has, confine yourself to growing only annuals (flowers or vegetables) in the affected area until you beat back the invader. Battling perennial weeds among perennial plants is logistically daunting. With severe infestations, you may have to remove all desirable plants in the area, no matter what they are, and then get to work and fight until you prevail.

Zone Matters

TEMPERATURES

$$°C = 5/9 \times (°F-32)$$
$$°F = (9/5 \times °C) + 32$$

Plant Hardiness Zones
Average Annual Minimum Temperature

ZONE	TEMPERATURE (DEG. F)	TEMPERATURE (DEG. C)
1	Below −50	Below −46
2	−50 to −40	−46 to −40
3	−40 to −30	−40 to −34
4	−30 to −20	−34 to −29
5	−20 to −10	−29 to −23
6	−10 to 0	−23 to −18
7	0 to 10	−18 to −12
8	10 to 20	−12 to −7
9	20 to 30	−7 to −1
10	30 to 40	−1 to 4
11	40 and above	4 and above

To see the U.S. Department of Agriculture Hardiness Zone Map, go to the U.S. National Arboretum site at http://www.usna.usda.gov/Hardzone/ushzmap.html.

Metric Conversions

INCHES	CM	FEET	M
¼	0.6	1	0.3
½	1.3	2	0.6
1	2.5	3	0.9
2	5.1	4	1.2
3	7.6	5	1.5
4	10	6	1.8
5	13	7	2.1
6	15	8	2.4
7	18	9	2.7
8	20	10	3
9	23	20	6
10	25	30	9
		40	12
		50	15
		60	18
		70	21
		80	24
		90	27
		100	30
		1000	300

Suggested Reading

Better Homes & Gardens. *Ask the Garden Doctor*. Des Moines, IA: Better Homes & Gardens, 2010.

Bradley, Fern Marshall. *Rodale's Vegetable Garden Problem Solver*. Emmaus, PA: Rodale Books, 2007.

Damrosch, Barbara. *The Garden Primer*, 2nd edition. New York: Workman Publishing, 2008.

Frowine, Steven A., and the Editors of the National Gardening Association. *Gardening Basics for Dummies*. Hoboken, NJ: Wiley Publishing, Inc., 2007.

Hill, Lewis. *Pruning Made Easy*. North Adams, MA: Storey Communications, Inc., 1998.

Lovejoy, Sharon. *Trowel and Error: Over 700 Shortcuts, Tips & Remedies for the Gardener*. New York: Workman Publishing, 2003.

Reader's Digest. *The Garden Problem Solver: The Ultimate Troubleshooting Guide for Successful Gardening*. Pleasantville, NY: Reader's Digest, 2004.

Swain, Roger B. *The Practical Gardener: A Guide to Breaking New Ground*. Boston: Little, Brown and Company, 1989.

Yeh, Tamson. *Can My Petunia Be Saved? Practical Prescriptions for a Healthy, Happy Garden*. Brentwood, TN: Cool Springs Press, 2006.

Online resources

Cornell University's Cooperative Extension Service
cce.cornell.edu/gardening/Pages/default.aspx

Dave's Garden
davesgarden.com

Gardener's Journal, the official blog of the employee-owners of Gardener's Supply Company
blog.gardeners.com

Learn to Grow
learn2grow.com

Missouri Botanic Garden
mobot.org

Washington State University Extension/The Garden Professors
sharepoint.cahnrs.wsu.edu/blogs/urbanhort/default.aspx

Index

WES DUNN

About the author

Teri Dunn Chace is a writer and editor of dozens of books, including *Flower Gardening, Beautiful Roses Made Easy, Outstanding Perennials, 100 Favorite Herbs*, and *Potting Places: Creative Ideas for Practical Gardening Workspaces*. She has also written and edited extensively for *Horticulture, North American Gardener, Backyard Living*, and *Birds & Blooms*. Raised in California and educated at Bard College in New York, Teri has gardened in a variety of climate zones and soil types, from inner city Portland, Oregon, to coastal Massachusetts. She now lives in a small upstate New York village with snowy winters and glorious summers.